"In a world f
the call to
desperately needed. David Fitch has provided a framework
of discipleship and mission that powerfully echoes the
life of Jesus and the best of Christian spiritual formation.
I have found the path that Fitch outlines quite formative
and powerful. The church is in urgent need of discerning
the way toward healing in our local communities and
the larger cultural landscape. *Seven Practices for the
Church on Mission* offers us the practices to help us do
just that."

Rich Villodas, lead pastor of New Life Fellowship Church,
Queens, New York City

"While missional might seem like a buzzword these days,
it's always been central to the call of the bride of Christ.
More than ever this is a conversation that all churches
should lean into. David Fitch offers practical ways for
ordinary Christians to order their lives to participate in
the mission of God. This book removes the intimidation
factor and helps readers discover that mission may not
be as daunting as they thought."

Tara Beth Leach, senior pastor of First Church of the
Nazarene, Pasadena, CA, author of *Emboldened*

"Seamlessly blending theological reflection, pastoral
narrative, and practical guidance, David Fitch has given
clergy and laity alike a field guide to missional, church-
based ministry that both edifies the body of Christ
and extends her life into the world for the sake of the
gospel."

Tim Keel, senior pastor of Jacob's Well, Kansas City, MO

"The American church needs to demonstrate its commitment to Jesus with actions. Despite efforts to gain influence through politics or through entertaining weekend services, the church has lost credibility, particularly among younger people. David Fitch has offered biblical and practical guidance for how churches can regain some credibility by being agents of transformation in their neighborhoods. This book has helped our church to see the Lord's Table as more than a ritual, to live more fully in our calling to be reconcilers, and has generally motivated us in our witness for Christ."

Dennis R. Edwards, senior pastor of Sanctuary Covenant Church, Minneapolis, MN

"*Seven Practices for the Church on Mission* reminds us that it's in the long-term communal devotion to small but transformative practices that our churches will discover and reflect the faithful presence of God."

Mandy Smith, lead pastor of University Christian Church, Cincinnati, OH, author of *The Vulnerable Pastor*

SEVEN
PRACTICES
FOR THE
CHURCH
ON
MISSION

DAVID E. FITCH

IVP Books

An imprint of InterVarsity Press
Downers Grove, Illinois

InterVarsity Press
P.O. Box 1400, Downers Grove, IL 60515-1426
ivpress.com
email@ivpress.com

*InterVarsity Press® is the book-publishing division of InterVarsity Christian
Fellowship/USA®, a movement of students and faculty active on campus at
hundreds of universities, colleges, and schools of nursing in the United States of
America, and a member movement of the International Fellowship of Evangelical
Students. For information about local and regional activities, visit intervarsity.org.*

*Scripture quotations, unless otherwise noted, are from the New Revised
Standard Version of the Bible, copyright 1989 by the Division of Christian
Education of the National Council of the Churches of Christ in the USA. Used by
permission. All rights reserved.*

*While any stories in this book are true, some names and identifying information
may have been changed to protect the privacy of individuals.*

*Paintings at chapter openings are by Catherine Lindloff, Peace of Christ Church,
Westmont, Illinois, and are used courtesy of Catherine Lindloff.*

Cover design: David Fassett
Interior design: Daniel van Loon
Image: Street map: © mattjeacock / iStockphoto

ISBN 978-0-8308-4142-4 (print)
ISBN 978-0-8308-8744-6 (digital)

Printed in the United States of America ∞

*InterVarsity Press is committed to ecological stewardship and to the
conservation of natural resources in all our operations. This book was printed
using sustainably sourced paper.*

Library of Congress Cataloging-in-Publication Data

A catalog record for this book is available from the Library of Congress.

P 25 24 23 22 21 20 19 18 17 16 15 14 13 12 11 10 9 8 7 6 5 4 3 2 1

Y 37 36 35 34 33 32 31 30 29 28 27 26 25 24 23 22 21 20 19 18

To the people of
Peace of Christ Community
of the
Christian and Missionary Alliance,
Westmont, IL

CONTENTS

PREFACE

Writing the book *Faithful Presence* was a transformative experience for me. Through studying the Scriptures and then writing this book, I more fully realized how central *presence* is to what God is doing in the world. Presence is the way God works. Through his presence, he is bringing the whole world to himself.

Our task then as Christians could be summarized in one short sentence: *Be present to his presence*. Having been restored to relationship with God through Jesus Christ, let us open space for his presence in our lives and for the people we encounter all around us. In all our relationships, let us discern his presence and cooperate with what he is doing.

But this is not as easy as it sounds. We need practices for discerning his presence.

In *Faithful Presence* I described how Jesus gave his disciples practices for opening space for his presence. These were directions on how to make

way for his kingdom to come among us, his salvation to break in. I illustrated how these practices
shape the way we live in our neighborhoods by
using three circles to describe three kinds of spaces
we all live in each week. We practice simple ways
of eating, praying, reconciling, and so forth in first
a close circle together. Then we do the same in our
neighborhood together and then among the hurting.
Each of the seven disciplines outlined in *Faithful
Presence* is to be practiced in this way. I contend
that the New Testament is full of evidence dis-
playing how this was a way of life for the first
church. And the Christian gospel spread around
the world. Could we again recapture these practices
as a way of life for today?

I have been grateful for how *Faithful Presence*
has been received among pastors and churches
around the world in its first year of publication.
As a result, many have asked me for a simpler
version of the seven disciplines in the book. Perhaps
I could produce a smaller version of this book that
trims some of the intense theology and focuses
only on the disciplines themselves. Maybe this
could be helpful in recapturing these practices for
church communities.

Perhaps this book could be published as a pocket
version that could be carried around and read in

those unforeseen moments during any given day when we have some free time. Perhaps it would be cheap enough to be distributed to congregations more broadly than the larger book. Perhaps such a book would get conversations going in a congregation or spur on an imagination that would enable us all to better live these disciplines again as they once were lived in the early church.

To this end, then, with some editorial help from InterVarsity Press, we have produced this pocket version of *Faithful Presence*. We hope it meets all these expectations.

Jesus, before he ascended, sent the church out with the words "All power in heaven and on earth has been given unto me." He alerted everyone that he is at work over the whole world bringing in his kingdom. And yet he promised "lo I go *with* you even until the completion of the age [or mission]" (Mt 28:18-20, my translation). I pray this little book can help train Christians everywhere to recognize and participate in Jesus' presence as he goes *with* us all the way to his mission being completed. Even so, come, Lord Jesus!

ONE

THE LORD'S TABLE

The Lord's Table is about presence. Surely it is about eating, but ultimately it's a practice that shapes a group of people to be present to God's presence in Christ around the table, where we eat. Then, in the process, we are able to connect with the other people around the table. Our lives are then reordered socially by his presence. This practice was inaugurated by Jesus himself and given to his disciples on "the night he was betrayed." Today, almost all Christians practice it. This first practice we explore shapes a community into God's faithful presence.

Though there are differences in the way Christians practice the Lord's Table, there is a common core to what we do together. All churches, for instance, incorporate the "words of institution" as the means to remember together the meaning of the bread and wine. "This is my body that is for you." "This cup is the new covenant in my blood. Do this, as often as you drink it, in remembrance of me" (1 Cor 11:24-25).

There is almost always a communal invitation to peace and reconciliation prior to the table. The presiding leader challenges all believers to make sure there is no enmity between us as we come to the table. There is almost always a prayer of thanksgiving (eucharist) and a blessing that inaugurates the celebration of the table. Usually the Holy Spirit is invited to this table, making possible the living and real presence of Christ at the meal. Then there is the actual breaking and distribution of the bread and the sharing of the cup. His broken body and shed blood becomes a meal we ingest into our bodies as the very basis of life itself. Last, an offering of material goods often is taken as part of the Lord's Table. We believe that this abundance shared around the table will flow forth from the table through the whole of our lives and then return all over again.

Now, let's try to understand how the table shapes us to know and discern God's presence among us and in the neighborhood.

DISCERNING HIS PRESENCE

When we sit around this table and tend to Christ's presence, our eyes are opened and we know his presence is here in a special way. The first reported time this happened post-resurrection was on the road to Emmaus when Jesus joined the two disciples on their walk (Lk 24). On this day of his resurrection, as they came near their village, they invited Jesus to join them in their home, which always meant a meal around a table. While they were at the table, Jesus "took bread, blessed and broke it, and gave it to them," and their eyes were opened to his presence with them (Lk 24:30-32). So also today Jesus' presence is "known . . . in the breaking of the bread" (Lk 24:35). Jesus' presence historically has been uniquely real and recognizable around the table.

Each of us must come to grips again with the reality that Christ is present at the table in a real, sacramental way. We must tend to his special presence because his presence always brings the reordering of our lives together into his kingdom. This is what makes this table so revolutionary at the core: here God shapes a people to be his kingdom in the world.

It's hard for evangelical Protestants to conceive that there is something unique happening around the table. Yet here we have perhaps the single best opportunity to train ourselves to tend to his presence for our lives. Here we can recognize and receive the forgiveness that flows from his broken body into our lives, the healing of reconciliation, the renewal of all things through the cup of the new covenant relationship we have with God the Father through the Spirit.

A KINGDOM IS BEING BORN

Around this table God's kingly rule over the whole world meets his incarnational presence in this particular time and space. There is no kingdom without subjects to the King, so we must begin by subjecting ourselves to him. As we submit to Christ's presence there, we are realigned into his reign. Our submission to Jesus spreads out into mutual submission to one another. And a new social order is birthed out of this, which is nothing less than his kingdom.

In John 13:1-17, Jesus gets down on his hands and knees and washes the feet of his disciples to demonstrate submission. He could not be more explicit about the way we will relate to one another in this kingdom. The whole scene prefigures the kingdom and points to the new world coming (Lk 22:30). This kingdom will be founded on mutual submission to one another under the lordship of Christ, where anyone who rules does so through submission to the work of God happening in the midst of us.

Think of how earthshaking this experience of Christ at the table must have been for the early Christians. The very presence of the risen Lord is here at this table. Something so special, even dangerous, is happening when they gather around it. It's a matter of life and death (1 Cor 11:29-30). Yet as each person submits to him, our relationships with one another and to Christ are opened up. The socioeconomic relationships among us are realigned as we share mutually out of what we have and what we receive.

In this space we submit all of our divisions and personal agendas to Christ's presence. All of this must die. There we sit, tending to one another and to his presence. And an amazing social dynamic breaks forth that can only be described as a new political order subverting all other allegiances. Just as the first tables of the early Christians subverted Rome and Caesar and started a new way of life before the watching world, so this table subverts all other politics of self-preservation, accumulation, and individualism. A profound flourishing in the kingdom results.

It is essential then that we lead one another into submission to Christ at the table. Because God will not impose himself on us or overwhelm us, our submission to his reign opens up space for him to work. The people who carry the most power must submit first, just as Christ did when he washed the disciples' feet. By example, the leader will lead the community into a place of submission to the one Lord and to one another under his lordship.

THE TABLE IN THE THREE CIRCLES

Most people think of the Lord's Table as being practiced only on Sunday mornings by committed Christians. But the life of Jesus and the pattern of the primitive church reveals multiple spaces where the table is practiced. These spaces can be summarized in terms of three circles: the close circle, the dotted circle, and the half circle.[1]

The Lord's Table in the close circle. The close circle represents the first space of the Lord's Table. We carefully discern our relationship to God in Christ before we dare approach it. Are we in full submission to Christ? Is there any enmity between me and someone else around this table? Because of this discernment, there is the closest of fellowship and unity with one another.

This closeness around the table is evident on the night when Jesus was betrayed. Here, at the celebration of the Passover, *Jesus is seated as the host*. He presides, and yet he washes his disciples' feet in a display of utter and total vulnerability. Intimate conversation is happening. The disciple "whom Jesus loved" reclines next to Jesus in closeness (Jn 13:23). And the one who eats the bread unworthily walks out in disdain, to his own doom (Jn 13:27-30). He cannot stand the intensity of the closeness. It is almost as if we are forced to deal with who we are and our submission to Jesus and his mission. The presence of Christ, by the Spirit, reveals our brokenness. It forces renewed commitment. It orders our lives intensely, either further into or away from the kingdom.

This closeness marks the table after Christ's ascension as well. In 1 Corinthians 11, Paul is shocked at the Corinthians' disregard for one another in Christ's presence. The Lord's presence there is so intense that they indeed get sick and die because they have disregarded him. This table therefore requires discernment. At this table the closest of fellowship is experienced with the resurrected Jesus.

The Lord's Table in the dotted circle. But the table doesn't stop there. It extends into the neighborhood. Here, around our neighborhood tables we gather to eat regularly. We start with Christian friends, and then, over time, our neighbors, as they look on, are welcomed around our tables. The dotted circle represents this second space for the table. It is constituted by Christians forming a circle of those submitted to Christ's presence. Yet there are openings in the circle, where strangers are welcomed in. So the circle is porous or dotted.

In this dotted circle the Christian in the world *becomes the host.* Typically, this table takes place in homes in neighborhoods. But it can happen wherever Christians meet regularly to share a meal in the hospitality of Christ's presence. This meal is initiated by a Christian, hosted by a Christian, and yet is always open and hospitable to strangers who are becoming regular parts of our lives. Christ's special presence is extended into the neighborhood.

In Mark 6:30-44 we see thousands of people gathering around Jesus. They were not yet part of the kingdom. In many ways this is a circle of

Christians ("the apostles gathered around Jesus" [v. 30]), yet with people "from all the towns" gathering as well. In other words, this is a dotted circle.

The disciples come to Jesus and report the need to send the crowds away so they can get something to eat. Jesus directs them in no uncertain terms to host the "table," saying, "You give them something to eat" (v. 37). Here is where the dynamic of the dotted circle kicks in.

The disciples immediately ask, "Are we to go and buy two hundred denarii worth of bread, and give it to them to eat?" (v. 37). They assume that they must do everything, take control, and provide out of their own resources. But this is not what it means for the Christian disciple to host the Table in the dotted circle. So Jesus shows them how to host. He asks them to bring him what food they have. Nothing more, nothing less. They find among the crowd five loaves and two fish, and bring it as an offering into the abundance of the kingdom in Jesus. He *takes* the loaves and fish, *blesses* and *breaks* them, and *gives* it to the disciples for distribution. These four words signal that this indeed is a Eucharistic celebration around the presence of Christ. In the midst of this meal, people meet the abundance of the kingdom as "all ate and were filled," and there was an abundance of food left over (vv. 42-43).

In this stunning story we see how the table extends the presence of Christ into places where curious onlookers are invited. We see that Christians are to host these tables. However, there is no presumption that all who partake are reconciled. Certainly the Christians around the table are practicing the reconciled life. But there is no discernment required of the onlookers. We send no one away, including people in conflict. We invite them to be with us among Christ. The host does not somehow take control of the table but facilitates the table around the presence of Christ, who reorders the world into his kingdom. The host allows the space to be opened for Christ to meet all our needs and more. This is what Christ was trying to teach his disciples at the feeding of the five thousand.

This dotted circle happened at our home every Friday night. Every one of us would bring food as our offering, place it in the kitchen, hold hands, gather as a circle, and pray a prayer of thanksgiving (eucharist) and invoking of Christ's presence (*epiklēsis*). Then we would sit and eat and talk. Sometimes the talk became egocentric and self-serving. Sometimes mayhem erupted as everybody scurried for attention or the need to be seen and heard. We would gently calm all this down, generously admonishing one another to be present and listen to the other person.

Some would move to another room and sit and talk while in front of the TV. They did not yet know or understand Eucharist. We had to make a rule: Everyone, no matter how many in the group, must always sit around the table. Smartphones were not allowed. We ate together, aware of the forgiveness, reconciliation, and renewal of all things that we had shared as a result of Sunday Lord's Table. As months rolled on, we learned how to be present with each other and to Christ among us. We discovered a different dynamic shared across a table between me and another person. It was the presence of Christ.

It took months to cultivate mutual submission and tending to Christ's presence. And I had to learn how to model as best I could a posture of submission and presence to each other and Christ around the table. (The one perceived in power always submits first.) When I spoke, it was to direct attention to someone other than myself, and (generally) I did not speak unless spoken to. It took months to cultivate trust, listening, and paying attention to the Spirit. A year later the presence around the table was so intoxicating, people's lives, attitudes, and physical health were transformed by the interactions.

At the time for dessert, the host would pose a question to center some conversation around what was going on in our lives. We sometimes focused on our personal lives or struggles with God, sometimes what was going on among us, and sometimes our lives with God in our neighborhood. The gifts of the Spirit were set into motion among us. After an hour or so, we all prayed, submitting these things to God and his kingdom. The presence of Christ became real among us as we became present to one another.

One time a couple in the neighborhood of one of our members was going through disruptive times with their teenage daughters. They knew about our Friday night group and wanted to attend. They were welcomed. In a way that was more comfortable than any of us had felt for the first six months of our table fellowship, they immediately began to share their wounds with us. I asked our guests if we could include them in our prayers. They hesitated, but said yes, and we did. They saw an unmistakable glimpse of the kingdom that night.

The Lord's Table in the half circle. The table however does not stop with the dotted circles of our neighborhoods. The table extends further through the half circle into the world, where the hurting and marginalized people live. Into these half circles Christians go, imitating Christ as he enters the homes of the outcast, the publicans, and the sinners. Here we no longer serve as hosts; instead, *we come as guests*, giving up all control. In all our weakness we submit to Christ's presence among us and allow him to work. We pay attention to what God is doing as we listen, tending to his work.

Something marvelous happens in this space. Christ's presence is here too. The question here however is, will he be recognized? Will Jesus be received? In Luke 10, Jesus sends the seventy-two into mission to "every town and place where he himself intended to go" (v. 1). He instructs them to enter a home and become present there, sitting around the table "eating and drinking whatever they provide" (v. 7). They are to go needy, be present as guests, and be vulnerable, "like lambs into the midst of wolves" (v. 3), giving up control. They are to take the posture of receiving before offering anything. They were not to move from house to house but to be present long enough to discover persons of peace (v. 6). In these postures of the guest, the space is opened for the presence of God in Christ to become manifest.

Jesus taught the seventy-two to sit with people around the table before he mentions proclaiming the gospel. Verses 8-9 say, "Eat what is set before you; cure the sick who are there, and [then] say to them, 'The kingdom of God has come near to you.'" So, as we sit *with* people, the occasion arises when the gospel will be proclaimed.

When we point to the kingdom and announce it is here, Jesus says, "Whoever listens to you listens to me, and whoever rejects you rejects me . . . [and] the one who sent me" (v. 16). Through the half-circle table then, the visible presence of Christ is extended. When Christ is received, when his lordship is submitted to, his presence is made visible; his kingdom comes.

One time my friend Gordon and I took an evening walk on the streets of Westmont, Illinois, where we live. As we walked the town's downtown streets, we stopped at the entrance to a bar and noticed the people gathered around tables drinking beverages; they were seeking communion. I was so struck by it I said to Gordon, "Look, there's Eucharist going on in that bar. It just hasn't been discerned yet." As we walked further, we noticed the same phenomena in the restaurants; the Magic gaming store, where teenagers gathered to play games; and Uncle Jon's Music, where people were playing banjo together.

In all these places we might be tempted to see only the signs of hunger and hurt. We easily recognized the brokenness because we see it and know it in our own lives. It was painfully obvious to Gordon and me how segregated the tables were. White people sat with white people, and Latinos with Latinos. Few African Americans were sitting in any of these places even though we had many black friends and acquaintances in the neighborhood. What was evident in all of these observations was the incompleteness at these tables. The fullness of Eucharist was missing.

Tragically, in many if not most of these places no one is tending to Christ. It takes someone who is there, who knows the stories around this table, who lives in Christ's presence, who knows his story, who can simply sit and be present, to recognize his presence. This is why the church must extend table awareness into the places of brokenness. This *presence* is what makes possible all proclamation of the gospel. This is what faithful presence requires.

THE CHURCH IS
ALL THREE SPACES TOGETHER

The Lord's Table happens every time we share a
meal together with people and tend to the presence
of Christ among us. Granted the formal Lord's
Table only happens at the close table. But that table
extends from there. The table is never merely *in
here* or *out there*. It is the continual lived space *with*
and *among* the world.

The three circles together are inextricably
linked. When we practice the table only as a closed
circle, we in effect close it off from the other two
circles, and the table becomes a maintenance
function of the church. In a similar vein, when
we practice the table as only the half circle in the
world, we in effect close off ourselves from discerning the presence of Christ in the world.
Devoid of Christ's presence in the world, the
church falls into exhaustion.

When we no longer practice the table in the
dotted circles of our lives, we lose the space to
extend Christ's presence as witness to our neighbors.
We lose the place where neighbors can be acclimated
to the ways of the kingdom. Rarely can a new believer go from the half circle directly to the close
circle. New believers must catch a glimpse of
normal, everyday kingdom life at the home in their

neighborhoods. From there they will go to the close circle. And in the end, if one is not to fall into either maintenance or exhaustion, every Christian, new or mature believer, must live in all three circles.

RECOVERING FAITHFUL PRESENCE
AROUND THE TABLE(S)

The church regularly defaults to maintenance mode. When the church gets overly comfortable in society, believing its place is secure in a Christian society, it is easy for a church to lose its mission. Likewise, when a church tries to defend its position against a society that is non-Christian, here too it can drift into doing the disciplines correctly and fall into maintenance mode.

The New Testament church, as best we can tell, practiced the table in all three circles as part of their everyday life together (Acts 2:46-47). There was a regular eating of the agape meal, which was differentiated from the Lord's Table (see Jude 12). These two practices together comprised the dotted table and the close table. In addition, the early church was known for its excessive hospitality in the neighborhoods—eating meals with the poor, the hurting, and sinners, and so we can conclude that the New Testament church, for at least its first two hundred years, functioned in all three circles of the Eucharist. And the kingdom of God was spreading throughout Rome.

In the fourth century, the Christian church was eventually sponsored by the Roman Empire. Millions of new believers were entering the churches. Somewhere along the line the practice of the table was organized for efficiency. It was taken out of the neighborhoods and brought into the church buildings. The leadership of the table shifted from the leaders among the people to the priest above the people. By the fifth century only the ordained priest could preside. We could say the table became managed for maintenance.

In fifteenth-century Europe, the focus of the presence of Christ around Eucharist moved from being in and among the community of the church around the table to being in the actual elements themselves on the table.[2]

Today, in evangelicalism, many churches practice the Lord's Table as a mere remembrance for a few short minutes after a Sunday morning service. We've lost the social reality that binds us together into the presence of Christ and the remaking of the world into his kingdom.

We therefore need to recover the table for the church's faithful presence in the world. Just as there have been countless other times when the church has fallen into maintenance (and exhaustion), only to find renewal around the table fellowships of its people, so we too can begin anew to intentionally reinvigorate the practice of the Lord's Table for mission in our churches today. Starting with the close-circle table, let us lead one another into the encounter with Christ's real presence. And then let's cultivate the practice of the table in our neighborhoods. Let's teach leaders how to tend to his presence at these tables by being present to one another. Then let's shape our people around the table to become guests among the tables of the hurting and lost. Let's lead people into a formative encounter with the living Christ at the table and then cultivate the extension of his presence into the rest of our lives. This is the beginning of faithful presence.

TWO

RECONCILIATION

Reconciliation is at the core of what God has done and is doing in the world in and through Jesus Christ. As the apostle Paul states,

> To all who are in Christ the new creation has begun, the old has passed away; behold all is becoming new. All this is from God, who reconciled us to himself through Christ, and has given us the ministry of reconciliation, that is, in Christ, God was reconciling the whole world to himself not counting their trespasses against them, but putting in us

the message of reconciliation. (2 Cor 5:17-19,
my paraphrase)

Reconciliation marks our presence in the world. It is so much a part of the gospel we bring into the world that the apostle Paul calls Christians "ambassadors" of his reconciliation (2 Cor 5:20).

For Jesus reconciliation is not merely an idea or a doctrine. It is something we do as his followers. More than a status given to us by God through Christ's work on the cross, it is what we practice together.

The practice is really quite simple. Jesus says, "If another member of the church sins against you, go and point out the fault when the two of you are alone" (Mt 18:15). Go privately and directly to the person who has hurt you. We are to listen and be listened to.

The offense presented could be a sin or simply a conflict between us as we seek to discern life together as a community. If we disagree on something important with someone, if we are in unresolved turmoil, we are told to express our grievance or disagreement and seek agreement.

If agreement or peace is not reached, Jesus instructs us to bring one or two more people into the conversation as witnesses. A space is now being formed among *us*. Jesus promises to be present in this space. In this space we seek clarity and eventual agreement. This may include repentance or mutual sharing of peace. All the while this space is determined by the good news that Jesus as Lord is working for his will in this conflict.

If agreement is still not reached, we take the disagreement to the community as a whole, which for some traditions means the elder or executive board, or perhaps a town hall meeting before all interested parties of the church (if indeed the matter affects the entire church). We will listen to the gifted ones, hear the gospel, and tend to each other and Christ's presence among us. We will say, "Based on Scripture, my prayer life, and what I know from last week, I believe God is saying _____, and I submit to you. Are you seeing what I am seeing?" We will use a consensus-based decision-making process guided by the Holy Spirit. We will stay at this mutual dialogue in mutual submission until all parties are satisfied that Christ Jesus has been followed and submitted to as Lord.

James 5:16 says, "Confess your sins to one another . . . that you may be healed [saved]." The Greek word for *confess* actually means to put your words out there in a space for agreement. We do this humbly in gentleness (Gal 6:1). When we do this, Christ's presence by the Spirit is unleashed among us, and he works to reconcile, heal, and discern the kingdom among us. The salvation of God is revealed.

The goal of this practice is not vindication or punishment. It is restoration, healing, and renewed common fellowship. It is the discerning of the future as the Spirit of Christ works among us. At the core of this practice is the presence of Christ established between two people (Mt 18:20). Listening grounds this practice. And so *presence* is central to it. Reconciliation is fundamentally a practice of faithful presence.

RECONCILIATION AS HIS KINGDOM

When we gather to reconcile, we gather in his name (Mt 18:20). Invoking the name of Jesus Christ in this way is no different than bowing to his reign or authority (e.g., Lk 10:17). He is recognized as Lord in this place. As people enter into this place under his authority, they are stripped of all presumption of power. The kingdom is being birthed here. We do not live as "the Gentiles do," "lording it over" one another.

Just as Jesus inaugurated the Eucharist by denouncing all posturing for position, so too here there is implied a mutual submission to the one Lord. This place between us is sacred ground for the kingdom. Here, in the midst of this dispute, a way forward will be revealed.

Jesus makes it plain that whenever two or more people go through this process and reach an agreement, the authority and power of the kingdom of heaven is unleashed (Mt 18:18). And so this is not a contest to see who will win. We in effect give up our interest in winning for the sake of something much greater, deeper, richer, and profound to occur in our midst: the reordering of our world for the kingdom to come.

At our church, the words "I submit to you" became all important in our discernments. No matter how firm our convictions, no matter how clearly we put forth where we believed God was leading, after we finished speaking, we looked into the other person's eyes and said, "I submit to you." Other words follow: "What am I not seeing?" "What would you do if you were me?" "Do you see it this way too, or differently?" As always, it is important for the one in perceived power to submit first to the one whose voice is heard less. Make space for the other voice.

In essence, submission opens up a space for the Spirit to work reconciliation, growth, and learning

what the future might look like. I can do this because I can trust that Jesus is Lord and is working
over this space. I do not have to fear among Christians, because, as we submit to Jesus as Lord and
not our own devices, I can give up all violence or
defense. I can submit to you. The fear of the
oppressed is eased here, and a space is cleared for
his presence. Christ's rule now begins to work for
the future of the world. This is what faithful
presence looks like.

KINGDOM AND PRESENCE

The practice of reconciliation, as with the Lord's
Table, presumes there is more going on here than
merely what happens between two or more persons
in a room. If we submit together to his name, Jesus
says, "I am there among [you]" (Mt 18:20). In this
practice a social reality is birthed where his presence
is sacramentally made real.

As a pastor I have encountered numerous conflicts within church life. It is an inevitable part of
life together. Sometimes when this happens, I am
asked to mediate, make a judgment between the
two people, and enforce it. I've learned that I must
reject this mode of operating. Instead, I must see
this moment as the opportunity to invite these
persons into the Holy of Holies, the very presence

of Christ. If I do mediate and make a judgment on the conflict, inevitably one person will leave the church and the other stay. If we submit together to what God is doing, God takes us together to somewhere new in our lives we could have never anticipated.

One time a newly widowed woman, Emily, in our church was overburdened with taking care of her two children, homeschooling them, while also holding down a job. Sylvia, who was a social worker, offered to help. She sacrificially gave many hours to working with Emily's children. One of the children had special needs, according to Sylvia. She believed that Emily was not taking care of the children's educational needs. After a few discussions with Emily about this, Emily asked Sylvia to not visit her children any longer. Sylvia, in a huff, reported Emily to the Department of Children and Family Services, charging Emily with neglect of her children.

The resulting breach of trust could not have been worse. When the pastors asked them to come together to mutually submit to Christ, we were refused. Emily told the pastors to get Sylvia "in line." Sylvia said it was her professional duty to report Emily to the proper authorities. She was an expert. There was no need for further discussion. Two more times we attempted to bring them together. The third time the pastors sat with each one and asked what they were afraid of. We talked about the kingdom and the way God works through his presence coming into these spaces. Nonetheless both Sylvia and Emily refused to give up the authority of their positions as parent and social service professional. They both left the church. And our church body was poorer. What would God have taught our church about leading our children if they had practiced reconciliation?

Disagreements, conflict, and even oppression are signs that we are engaging challenging places with the gospel. Churches in mission should welcome disagreements as signs that God is moving and that he comes to be present among us. They are signs of faithful presence.

RECONCILIATION IN THE THREE CIRCLES

As with the Eucharist, practicing reconciliation follows the pattern of starting with the close circle and moves into all areas of the community's way of life.

Reconciliation in the close circle. In Matthew 18 we catch a glimpse of the close circle of reconciliation. Jesus directs the offended person to literally go to "your brother," a word Jesus often uses to refer to his close group of disciples. Jesus implies the person is a family member. In fact the prior verse (v. 17) is one of the few times Jesus uses the word *church*. So there is little doubt that Jesus intended this practice to be an intense part of the close circle of Christian life.

In 1 Corinthians 5 we discover some dynamics peculiar to the close circle of reconciliation. Evidently, a man in the close circle is living in sexual relationship with his father's wife. Paul calls for extreme measures. Just as with the Lord's Table, the close circle of reconciliation demands discernment. If anyone refuses to submit to one another under Christ's reign, this is to be made visible so that everyone within the close circle can see it and discern it. In both Matthew 18:17 and 1 Corinthians 5:3-5, the community is instructed to make visible the refusal of one's submission to one another in reconciliation under Christ's name. In 1 Corinthians 5:3-5 the apostle makes explicit that this is a communal act, and as we are present with each other, we discern expulsion.

Reconciliation in the dotted circle. The practice of reconciliation does not stay in the close circle. And so when we take up table fellowship in the neighborhood, we must assume that reconciliation extends there as well. We submit to each other under Christ during the week in the same way as we do on Sundays or within church polity.

It was not uncommon on a Friday night at our house for a conflict to break out. We'd be eating around the large table, tending to one another and one thing would lead to another, and someone would burst out with an accusation against someone at the table. The tension was palpable. Nonetheless, we were able to submit and listen. There would be a nonanxious presence in the room. The aggrieved person would air out their struggle and pain. Some ugly assumptions would be hurled. Then slowly either the person voicing the conflict or the one being accused (or another person around the table) would say something like, "George, I love you, and here is the way I see things. I submit to you. Does that make any sense?" or "I never saw that before. I repent of my pride. What can I do to show you I care and love you as a brother (or sister) in Christ?" Over the months we saw some antagonisms unwind, some resentments disappear, some binding oppressions lifted, some people's lives healed. The kingdom was breaking in.

The practice of reconciliation extends into everyday life. But it is always preceded by presence. Christians hosting other Christians are to see themselves as hosts of reconciliation in everyday life.

And as we live this reconciled life before our neighbors, people begin to see how we deal with conflict, how we engage cultural and racial prejudices among us, how our marriages carry on and grow through conflict, how our lives with one another grow even though we are so starkly different from one another. And the neighbors down the street, those struggling with marital or racial conflict, those at war with their city or police, begin to see a new way of living. They become curious and ask how this is possible. They slowly become drawn into the world of the kingdom alive in their neighborhood.

Reconciliation in the half circle. Like the Eucharist, the practice of reconciliation does not stay located among dotted circles of our neighborhoods. It is extended by Christians into the places we live and intersect with non-Christians, the half circles of our lives, where we are guests. As we seek to inhabit the places of racial injustice, violence and addiction, economic injustice, and family brokenness, we tend to Christ's presence. As we share meals around tables and inhabit other places of faithful presence, opportunities arise for Christians to offer the way of reconciliation as a gift from Christ to the world.

Every neighborhood, social gathering, and meeting place is a flowing stream of antagonistic broken relationships. As we sit and tend to Christ's presence among these various places of life, the occasion will arise to offer the reconciliation of God in Christ for the whole world. We cannot predict whether the offer will be received. Instead, we sit humbly and vulnerably, listening with the compassion of Christ. And as we do, Jesus becomes present. And the occasion comes to offer reconciliation in this excessively tangible way: "I believe I have wronged you" or "I believe my forbearers have wronged you." "I repent from these wrongs." "How can I work with you to make these things right?" As I have learned from many friends of color in the Black Lives Matter movement, sometimes reconciliation can only begin with the confession that something very wrong was done and that I have been a part of it.

In the midst of a broken relationship, the practice of reconciliation can also offer something like, "I believe Jesus has forgiven all the wrongs in this room. You all are forgiven in him. He wants to come and be present here to reconcile. Can we seek forgiveness? Can the wrongs be set right?" Again, Christ can be rejected. This is the nature of the half circle. But if we start with being present to each other and then to Christ's presence, Christ himself can be welcomed. The kingdom can become visible. People's lives are transformed. In opening this space for Christ, an entry ramp has been formed into Christ's kingdom.

Christ announces in the Sermon on the Mount, "Blessed are the peacemakers, for they will be called children of God" (Mt 5:9). He is describing life in the in-breaking kingdom via the half circle. The beatitudes are blessings on those who live in the kingdom, and yet they also infer we are living in the world. This beatitude is not saying "blessed are peaceful," but "blessed are the ones who are at work making peace." The blessings of the kingdom are on those practicing reconciliation in the world. Christians are therefore to live in such a way that the half circle of reconciliation is always open.

TOWARD RACIAL RECONCILIATION

Some may say that the practice of reconciliation is too small of a strategy to make an impact on the systemic injustices of our day. We must fight through larger organizations and governmental strategies.

I would never want to discourage such larger efforts. But in order for such efforts to avoid becoming another bumper sticker or a T-shirt slogan, they must be shaped by practicing the face-to-face presence Jesus teaches us in Matthew 18:15-20. The various mass efforts for justice of the past century have shown a propensity to be absorbed into our societal systems. Civil rights legislation has at times become the means to institutionalize racism through other means. Injustice can so easily become justified by an ideology that enables the privileged to point to the injustice, make minor changes, control it, and move on.

And so Christians are called to be present in the half circles of injustice, broken racial relationships, the oppression of one person by another. A public demonstration, done in peace, can orchestrate such a face-to-face encounter. The victims, as well as people standing with the victims, become present to the oppressor. The march puts real human faces on the injustice. A moment of presence then occurs, and it becomes extremely uncomfortable for the privileged to turn their faces away and move on. A space is opened to dislodge the ideology and invite the oppressor to submit to one another. Repentance and reconciliation can begin.

The idea of bodily face-to-face *presence* here is key. In Martin Luther King Jr.'s words, it will be nonviolent with the goal of creating a "constructive non-violent tension" in the minds of the public versus a "violent tension."[1] This constructive nonviolent tension is presence. It is necessary and inevitable as we seek to bring the reconciliation of God in Christ into the world. It is dangerous. Christ was crucified and Martin Luther King Jr. was assassinated in this tension. But thus is the beginning of true reconciliation. It is the opening of space for the presence of Christ and the actual practice of reconciliation.

FAITHFUL PRESENCE AND
THE RECONCILIATION OF THE WORLD

One evening in October, while sitting in front of the neighborhood ice cream shop, I met a Latino man named Jorge. He told me stories of the police giving him tickets for his car being parked over the sidewalk. This man felt it was a "white man's law" written for Westmont people living as single families. Because Latino people often live three families to a house, they had more cars. White people lived more often as single-family households. The sidewalk parking law was therefore a white man's law because it discouraged Latino people and other less affluent people from living in Westmont. That evening we talked about the built-in racism of our town. We pledged that day to work together for peace.

That began a journey for me to more awareness of the racial divides of my suburb of Westmont. A few weeks ago, while writing this chapter, four police cars stopped one black man in front of our house. With a new awareness, I decided in all my white machismo to do something about it. So I called a meeting. I said to our leadership, "Let's bring our black, Latino, Asian, and white brothers and sisters together and have a meeting! Let's invite some police officers. Let's talk about this, listen to each other, work for peace." Let's open up space for the kingdom. Let's lead some reconciliation!

Jean, a woman leader in our church, looked at me graciously and said, "Dave, you're doing it again." I said, "What? Doing what?" She said, "You're doing your white privilege thing. You're inviting people of color to come to your church building to settle a problem. You are taking a posture of power. You are leading the meeting. You are enforcing your rule on them." She said I somehow needed to get invited to their turf. They need to invite me into these struggles. She was telling me I needed to be present long enough to be a guest, and offer, as opposed to impose, reconciliation. This is the way God brings healing. This is the way faithful presence works.

My knee-jerk response was, "That could take years." I thought to myself how much I would have to order my life differently so that I could be among these friends and spend time being present to them. I must sacrifice time, speaking engagements, nights watching hockey games. I must be present to them on their terms and watch basketball or soccer ("football") games. I must be present regularly over time. When and if the time comes, I must offer to our neighborhood the reconciliation that God is working in the world through Jesus Christ.

Imagine what could happen if churches everywhere inhabited their neighborhoods with Christ's faithful presence of reconciliation. Amid domestic disputes on the block, gang fights in the local school, racist police activities on my street, we bring a concrete practice of reconciliation that begins with presence. As we become present at local tables, protest marches, every conflict in our churches, with faithful presence, imagine what God might do. According to Jesus this is how the world will change. God in Christ is reconciling the whole world to himself (2 Cor 5:19), and we are his ambassadors (v. 20).

THREE

PROCLAIMING
THE GOSPEL

We are told daily, via media statistics, that few can escape the cycles of poverty. Socioeconomic circumstances dictate our future. Psychologists tell us people don't change. Addictions never go away; they can only be managed. Problems can only be manipulated by science, but never transcended. Social problems can only be changed through government, and the government is corrupt. As a result, most modern North Americans see situations in terms of either we make things happen or there can be no change. We must take control. And when there is no possibility for such control, we feel helpless. Our lives are traps we cannot get out of.

We are a society that yearns for hope. We crave good news of healings and restoration. We long for the gospel, for a new world to be born.

PROCLAIMING THE GOSPEL

But how will this new world be born? How will the seeds of hope fund the imagination and space be opened up so that we can see God at work and join in with him?

In places where Jesus is not recognized as Lord, we are told every day our ultimate identity is the success of our careers, our economic status, our bodies, the things we own or consume, the success of our children. We are put in despair whenever any of these things does not go as planned. And so it takes hearing the good news regularly to live into the reality that Jesus is Lord and working all things for his mission. Only then can our minds be formed, our imaginations shaped, so as to live daily in this reality. Proclaiming the gospel is the power from which God births salvation to those who believe (Rom 1:16). We must therefore regularly hear the gospel, submit to it, and faithfully respond to it if we would truly live in the reality of Christ's power. The heart of the church's life together is funded by the proclamation of the gospel.

WHAT IS THE GOSPEL?

What is the gospel? What does it mean to proclaim the gospel?

As the apostle Paul defines it, the gospel is the announcement that God has fulfilled the promise of the Scriptures to make the world right in Jesus Christ (1 Cor 15:1-11). Christ has died for our sins. By his death and resurrection (and ascension), he has defeated the effects of our sins, including death itself. He now sits at the right hand of the Father ruling over the world. In Christ the new creation has begun. Old things are passing way. Behold, the new has begun (2 Cor 5:17). All who respond to this good news, repent of the old ways, and make Jesus their Lord and Savior, enter in and become part of what God is doing to reconcile the whole world to himself (2 Cor 5:18-19), and receive power to become the children of God (Jn 1:12).[1] This in one paragraph is the gospel.

Personal salvation is certainly part of this gospel. But personal salvation alone is not the gospel. Certainly, in Christ we are pardoned, forgiven for our sins, and restored to a new relationship with

God the Father. This is all part of the gospel: God reconciling the whole of creation to himself. Certainly, in Christ we no longer fear death and know we will be raised with him. But the gospel is much bigger than that. The gospel is that God has come in Christ, who has been made Lord, and a whole new world (the kingdom of God) has begun. In Christ, God has begun to make all things right.

Proclaiming the gospel therefore is the art of announcing to our neighbors that this new world has begun in Christ.

PROCLAMATION VERSUS TEACHING

Proclaiming the gospel is a different kind of speech-act than most of us are used to. It accomplishes something different from conveying information. *Teaching* is moral instruction to Christians for how to live. It is the exposition of key beliefs. It may even be apologetics, helping the Christian to make sense of a belief in light of the world. But *preaching* is the public proclamation of the gospel. It is the announcement of a new world.

Proclamation is description. It is like painting a picture. The proclaimer describes the world as it is under Jesus as Lord and then invites the person into it. Proclamation does not explain the gospel or argue for it. Proclamation tells the story, describes the alternative account of reality it offers, and then asks, "Can you see it? Can you receive the news? Do you want to enter in?" The teacher then explains it by answering questions delving deeper into all its meanings. Christians need both proclamation and teaching.

Only after having seen the beauty of the story, the power of its description, being compelled by the reality of Christ's reign and "cut to the heart" by its goodness, can we ask, "What should we do?" (Acts 2:37). Only after having entered into the gospel can teaching make sense of what we now believe. Our lives respond in faith, choosing to enter the world as it is under his lordship. We then must learn more about what this world means.

The gospel does not come as "plausible words of wisdom," as a good teaching lesson. Instead it derives from "a demonstration of the Spirit and of power" (1 Cor 2:4). The authority of preaching does not derive from a person's expertise in biblical knowledge, reasons for believing, or rhetoric, although these skills may be of help. Proclamation is spoken from a place of weakness and humility (1 Cor 2:3). It tells the gospel from a place of having witnessed it, seen it, been humbled by it. It is unsettling. It calls for conversion (a response) every time.

In Luke 4, Jesus stands up in the synagogue and reads the famous passage from Isaiah, "The Spirit of the Lord is upon me." When he had finished all the eyes were fastened on him. His presence among them was riveting. He then proclaims, "Today this Scripture has been fulfilled in your hearing" (Lk 4:21 NASB). Luke takes notice of how "gracious" his words were (v. 22). His presence was gentle, not coercive. Nonetheless, this proclamation of the gospel birthed a new reality among them. More than a truth read or explained, proclaiming the gospel opens space for a new reality to be birthed among us by the Spirit. In our hearing and receiving it, it births a new reality in our midst.

The regular proclamation of the gospel makes possible the birth of a community living in the new world of his reign. It funds our ability to see God at work in all we're going through in our everyday lives. It brings us together to discern life in the new world under the one "mind of Christ" (1 Cor 2:16).

PRESENCE IN PROCLAMATION

As with the Eucharist and reconciliation, the practice of proclaiming the gospel opens space for Christ to be present among us. It clears space for Christ to come, be present, and transform all people in that space. Jesus states, after sending his disciples to proclaim the gospel of the kingdom into the towns and villages, that "whoever listens to you listens to me, and whoever rejects you rejects me, and whoever rejects me rejects the one who sent me" (Lk 10:16). In hearing and receiving, or hearing and rejecting, the gospel, Jesus is there. His power and authority breaks in by the Spirit. It is nothing short of "a demonstration of the Spirit and of power" (1 Cor 2:4). It is an event that opens space for Christ's presence. As with Eucharist and reconciliation, proclaiming the gospel shapes us into faithful presence in the world.

The preacher, therefore, at the Sunday gathering, must tend to the presence of Christ amidst the community, for it is in submission that the proclamation becomes the means of his power. The preacher must not stand over the community but must stand as one among the community being present to the people in the community's midst, for it is in this space that Jesus is found. From this posture comes the practice of proclamation. This is not a rhetorical performance. This is proclamation of the gospel for the people gathered in Christ's name in this space and in this time. In this way, in the close circle of the gathered community, preaching is an exemplary act of faithful presence.

SUBMISSION IN PROCLAMATION

The practice of proclaiming the gospel therefore invites the participant to submit, not to the preacher but to Jesus as Lord. This space of his subjects, both proclaimer and hearer, in submission to him opens the space for his reign, and we are able to hear the voice of God. The kingdom breaks in. As opposed to a response of pondering the pastor's eloquent, well-crafted words of wisdom (1 Cor 2:5), proclamation creates the conditions for either submission or rejection. Proclamation cannot be argued or debated, only accepted or rejected.

Proclaiming the gospel is a profoundly decentering experience that places the hearer in submission to God. It is the opposite of being in control. Proclaiming the gospel starts with, "Are you hopeless? Are you caught in a world gone wrong? Have you become caught up in sin? Are you powerless? Are you being destroyed by the world, by injustice?" It then moves to proclaiming that "God has come in Jesus Christ and defeated the powers. God has made Jesus Lord. He therefore rules and is working in all of your circumstances, personal and in the world. Will you give up control, submit to Jesus as Lord, and participate in this new world? Will you discern what it means to follow him (and join him) in his work of making the world right? Welcome to his kingdom."

PROCLAIMING THE GOSPEL ON THE MOVE

For Paul, the proclamation of the gospel is an ongoing part of the life of Christians and forms us regularly into the kingdom of God. Proclaiming the gospel therefore is not only for the people outside of Christ in the half circle. It must be part of the whole of Christian life, including the worship gathering and everyday life in the neighborhoods. It must take place in all three circles of our lives: the close, dotted, and half circles.

Proclamation in the close circle. Proclaiming the gospel, for most Christians, happens every Sunday in the close circle of the gathered community. The story is unfurled. Our minds are opened by the Spirit, and we are invited, right then and there, to live into this world where God is at work making all things right. And from there the gathering partakes of the eucharistic meal. We enter the kingdom together. A new world is being born. Proclaiming the gospel each Sunday grounds the church in the world as it is under

Jesus as Lord. As I like to say, I'm getting saved every Sunday morning.

During the first years of Life on the Vine Community's existence, we reflected seriously on the whats, whys, and hows of preaching. Why even have preaching? Few people remembered what we taught on any given Sunday anyway. Those who did rarely did anything with it. During this questioning, I began to see the difference between teaching and preaching. This differentiation began to reshape what we did in those twenty-five or so minutes when we would preach. I saw how important it was to proclaim weekly out of Scripture what God had done and is doing in and among us and through Jesus Christ. I saw how important it was to declare all of Scripture: what God has made possible in the life, death, and resurrection of Jesus Christ.

Proclaiming the gospel is always contextual. It is always grounded in our ability to be present with the people we are proclaiming it *over*.[2] We proclaim the kingdom because we have been sent to this place (Lk 10:1; Rom 10:15), and so it's always spoken out of where we have been called to live. So, as Life on the Vine community learned what proclaiming the gospel was, we discovered how important it was for preachers to stand among the congregation, present in their weakness (1 Cor 2:3), owning who they are, yet not making the sermon about them. From this posture we proclaimed the gospel for this people for this time. Then, instead of an application point, we offered the opportunity to respond. We offered sentence responses of confession, affirmation of truth, praise, submission to God, a step of faith, and obedience. We all bowed before his real presence, with each person offering a sentence prayer response that transported us into his kingdom.

Proclamation in the dotted circle. But the proclamation of the gospel does not stay in the close circle. It happens throughout the week in our neighborhoods. Just as we learn to hear the gospel proclaimed and respond to it in the close circle, we must now become proclaimers ourselves in our own houses and neighborhoods. The gospel must be proclaimed house to house in every context.

It all sounds so unnatural at first. It seems so foreign to proclaim the gospel to each other sitting around a table in a neighborhood. But just as with the close circle, so also in the home, we must first tend to being present to each other and to Christ's presence among us. As we sit around a table and share our lives with each other, expose our sufferings and our joys, a moment comes that begs

for the proclaiming of the gospel into our lives.
And so we must wait and listen, and when the time
is right, we might even ask humbly, "May I say
something?" And then, as with the first disciples,
the Holy Spirit guides us into all truth (Jn 16:13).

This gospel will be contextualized in this space
that is opened up in the neighborhood. There is
no one set gospel starting point. There are numerous
entry points. To the one suffering fear and anxiety,
Jesus is Lord, and he is working in that situation.
Can you believe and take a step forward in faith?
To the one angry at what has been done, Jesus is
Lord, vengeance is his, and he is working to reconcile all things. Can you forgive in Christ? To the
one suffering depression, God is working here,
he alone has created you for purposes before the
founding of the world. To the one who is lost in
guilt and shame, he has taken your sin in the cross
and forgives you unconditionally. He is Lord. Can
you receive that? To the one who is broken, he
heals; to one who is dying, we cannot be separated
from his love. Christ's lordship over the world may
be proclaimed over that addiction destroying someone's life. He is Victor. He is Lord in that broken
marriage and the evil cycle of violence that has got
ahold of our playgrounds in the neighborhood.
"Jesus is Lord" is the gospel. He is working for the

renewal of all things. Can we enter in, trust him, and begin to participate and discern what God is doing, and be faithful to him?

Every day in our neighborhoods, amid strife, broken relationships, and tragedy, whether we are Christians or not, we need the gospel. Christians must play host to spaces where the gospel can be proclaimed. As we gather around tables and the various meeting places of our lives, if we will be patient and tend to Christ's presence among us, the moments will *present* themselves for the gospel to be proclaimed contextually and humbly out of our own testimony. And in these moments Christ will be present, transformation will come, and onlookers will catch a glimpse of the kingdom. This is faithful presence.

Proclamation in the half circle. In Luke 10:1-16, Jesus gave to the disciples his most explicit instructions on proclaiming the gospel. He tells them to first go into the villages and be present with people. Go to be among them in their homes. Go without power, as lambs among wolves. Go needy, without money ("Carry no purse" [v. 4]). The disciples go as guests. Don't move from house to house. Instead be present, submit, eat what is offered, be a guest, put yourself at the mercy of the order and relationships in this place. In other words, be present. Only after these many instructions on being present does Jesus then instruct his disciples to proclaim the gospel.

It is therefore important to get the order straight. Just as in the close circle and the dotted circle, the one who proclaims must first be present. Presence precedes proclamation. Our tending to Christ's presence in the world, and to each other's presence, makes possible the proclamation of the gospel into people's lives. It is at the heart of faithful presence.

Just as in the other circles, the gospel must be proclaimed contextually in and among a person's life. For many of us in the secular world, when someone speaks of God, we ask, "Which one?" If someone talks about sin, many have never heard of such a thing. When we say "the Bible says," some might respond, "I'm happy you have found something that works for you." And so now we must be present, listening long enough until a space opens up where we can proclaim the gospel in words that make sense in the same humble posture we learned in the other two circles.

Proclaiming the gospel opens space for the inbreaking power and authority of Christ's reign. If the gospel is received, disruptions occur, signs and wonders of this new world follow. In the book of Acts we see that miracles accompanied the apostles when they proclaimed the gospel. And many entered into the kingdom. In the words of the apostle Paul, "My speech and my proclamation were not with plausible words of wisdom, but with a demonstration of the Spirit and of power" (1 Cor 2:4). And so the proclaimers of Luke 10 reported to Jesus, "Even the demons submit to us!" (v. 17). And Jesus replies, "I watched Satan fall from heaven like a flash of lightning" (v. 18). Satan had been dethroned from power. Proclaiming the gospel opens up space that demonstrates the power and authority of Christ's rule. This too is faithful presence.

And yet Jesus says, "Do not rejoice at this, that the spirits submit to you, but rejoice that your names are written in heaven" (v. 20). Don't think this demonstrates your power to control. Rejoice instead that you have been privileged to be participants in the power and authority of heaven itself, the seat of God's rule.

Despite these signs of the kingdom, when we proclaim the gospel in the half circles of our lives, where we live as guests, we always enter humbly, submitting to his presence. In submitting to the King, we open space for the kingdom. And so the apostle Paul makes it clear that in his proclaiming the gospel to the Corinthians, "I came to you in

weakness and in fear and in much trembling"
(1 Cor 2:3). He came not with brilliant words of
worldly wisdom but in humility. This is the posture
of the half circle. This is the posture that makes
possible the proclamation of the gospel as a guest.

RECOVERING FAITHFUL PRESENCE
IN A WORLD WITHOUT HOPE

A pattern through church history is that proclaiming the gospel becomes less prevalent whenever
the church gets comfortable in society. No longer
seeing the world as outside of Christ's reign, the
church turns its focus to teaching. It turns to deep-
ening the knowledge of its parishioners. This is
what Christendom does to the church. I have called
this the maintenance mode of the church.

When the church became the recognized religion
of Rome (after AD 378), historians report that the
practice of proclaiming the gospel diminished. The
church was consolidating and organizing for
the large populations coming into its membership.
The teaching office was formalized to keep some
control over deviant teaching. One cleric was now
responsible for all the teaching in one parish. Proclamation of the gospel was moved away from the
neighborhoods and into the homily at the Sunday
gathering in the church building.

When this happens, the gospel, as shaping the new world among us, gets lost. Expository teaching alone cannot fund imagination for what God is doing in the world. It is all a sign that the church is living out Christendom habits, keeping existing Christians reinforced in their current version of Christianity.

Sometimes proclaiming the gospel can get replaced with rally speeches for social justice causes or self-help speeches on how Jesus can help us lead an improved and more fulfilled life. There is a sense we are trying to bring in the new world ourselves. These are the signs that we have separated proclaiming the gospel from presence: both our presence among the broken and hurting, and Christ's presence with us. Exhaustion lies not far behind.

In order to avoid either maintenance or exhaustion, the church must recover the practice of proclaiming the gospel in all three circles. This starts with Christians being present to one another in the close and dotted circles of our lives, and learning to proclaim the gospel into each other's lives. This will shape our preaching on Sunday morning and our table fellowships in the neighborhood. This will subsequently shape a faithful presence in what God is doing in all the circles of our lives.

FOUR

BEING WITH THE
"LEAST OF THESE"

The world operates by people doing things for
and to people and then making them into projects.
This is an overstatement, I am sure. But it speaks
to the way American society organizes whole
systems to employ power efficiently, to get things
done at a price. Corporations hire consultants
to solve problems by recommending strategies
to be implemented by managers. Money flows to
put the solutions into motion. People are
employed by the managers to do things for people
at a price.

In this world, people become pieces to be managed within projects. And then people themselves become projects. Those who control the money control the power. We feel ourselves being categorized as we answer the questionnaire and then sit down for the job interview. We feel like a number as we wait in line and fill out forms to get food-stamp assistance at the local Department of Humans Services office. It's a dynamic we feel any time we sit across the desk from our supervisor at work for our year-end review. We agree that things like organization, accountability, and leadership are necessary, and yet something is missing. We imagine a world where each person is respected by every other person for what each one brings, where we all join together and share a kinship in an endeavor. The world, however, makes pawns of us all. We persevere nonetheless, all the while desiring something more. What we desire is kinship.

There is an inherent kinship in gathering people in the presence of Jesus. Jesus says as much when he tells his disciples, "I do not call you servants any longer, because the servant does not know what the master is doing; but I have called you friends, because I have made known to you everything that I have heard from my Father" (Jn 15:15). Later, when Jesus is told at a gathering that his mother and brothers want to speak to him, he answers, "Who is my mother, and who are my brothers?" And stretching out his hand toward his disciples, he says, "Here are my mother and my brothers! For whoever does the will of my Father in heaven is my brother and sister and mother" (Mt 12:48-50). In Christ's new kingdom no one becomes an object to or a project of someone else. We are invited to participate in life together with God. This is life lived in *withness*, kinship, faithful presence with one another.

This posture of being "with" is the signature mark of the way God has come to us in the world. "'The virgin shall conceive and bear a son, and they shall name him Emmanuel,' which means, 'God is with us'" (Mt 1:23). This is the posture we learn at the Eucharist and practice in reconciliation and proclaiming the gospel. But it is also a deliberate discipline we are called to practice regularly with the hurting, the impoverished, and the broken, those called "the least of these" (Mt 25:40). In this posture spaces are opened up among us for the in-breaking power of God in Christ. This is his kingdom.

BEING WITH THE LEAST OF THESE

Being with the "least of these" is a practice that shapes whole communities into Christ's kingdom. It starts by coming alongside hurting persons. This is something we do as a regular part of our lives as followers of Jesus. We are present to the other person and tend to the presence of Christ between us. In so doing, a space is opened where no one is over the other person, no one is an object, no one is a project.

From this space of kinship, we pray together, confess sin together, proclaim the gospel into each others' lives, share resources as needed, reconcile, speak truth in love, encourage one another. Being with "the least of these" is the practice of opening this space of withness between us and the poor, and tending to the presence of Christ there in that space. This space is like a clearing in the middle of a forest, where something new can be planted and new things can grow. And the authority of Jesus' reign comes rushing in by the Spirit. Being with the least of these is a practice fundamental to shaping communities in mission.

The early Christians were known for this. They walked the streets tending to and being with the poor. In the first centuries of the church this practice became regularized in the church via almsgiving. These Christians became known to the Roman authorities for the way they came alongside the poor, took them into their lives, and cared for their own orphans, widows, and poor. In early church history the church believed they were encountering the presence of the living Christ in the poor. It drove their existence.

The church is called to make being with the "least of these" a practice wherever the poor and hurting are found. It is a practice of community that opens up space for the presence of Christ to become visible. In these spaces we enter as people who come alongside. We come to be *with*. We come to discern. We come to be present. We come ready to give witness. We tend to his presence. The practice of being with the "least of these" is at the core of what it means to be God's faithful presence in the world. It is how God changes the world.

NOT A PROGRAM

Often we seek to make the poor into a program, persons we distribute resources to. Churches dedicate whole ministries to do justice and mercy as programs for the poor. They organize the ministries so people can volunteer to help. While such ministries alleviate immediate suffering, they inevitably keep the poor at a distance. They keep the poor from being a part of our lives. They prevent us from being present with the poor at our tables. In so doing, justice programs (done singularly) undercut God's work for justice in the world. They work against the new socioeconomic order God is creating in his kingdom.

In the parable of the final judgment found in Matthew 25:31-46, the Son of Man, having returned to gather his kingdom, separates the sheep from the goats, those who inherit the kingdom from those who don't. The sheep are welcomed into the kingdom based on the fact that they gave the Son of Man food to eat when he was hungry, a cup of water when he was thirsty, welcomed him when he was a stranger, clothed him when he was naked, and visited him in prison. Those who didn't do these things were sent into the eternal flames (v. 41). The righteous react with "Huh? When did we do that? We have no recall?" To which the King replies, "Truly, I say to you, as you did it to one of the least of these my brothers, you did it to me" (v. 40 ESV).

Jesus seems to be making the point that the righteous are unaware they were doing anything special when they were with the hurting. It appears that being with the poor was part of their everyday life. With no pretention, no worldly power or mammon, simply out of their everyday life, these people gave food to the hungry, a cup of water to the thirsty. They were with them. They were doing things they would do naturally for any friend or relative. They were in essence with kin. This is what it means to become present to the poor in our lives.

Jesus is emphasizing the relationship of the kinship God is calling us into with the poor. *Brothers* is about the family relationship (like Mt 12:49-50), being *with* the poor in such a way that we become family. Our relationship with the poor is not to be organized as a program at our local church. Instead, in everyday life we are to come alongside, be present to the poor in a relationship of family. In this relational space Jesus becomes especially present (when you did these things to one of the least of these my brothers, you did it to me—I was there [Mt 25:40]). Antagonisms become unwound. Resources are shared back and forth. Healing takes place. Relationships are restored. And a new world is born. This practice of being with the "least of these" is to characterize our everyday life as Christians, as Christ's church.

Church programs to alleviate pain and suffering, and to preserve the person through suffering, are important and should not be abolished! But the church must not be deluded into thinking these programs will redeem the world. More central to the church's life with the poor is the practice of being *with* the "least of these" as part of everyday life. Through history the church has made its biggest impact when it has practiced being with the poor and resisted turning the poor into a program.

A NEW WAY OF DOING ECONOMY

We should be careful whenever we distribute resources at a distance, apart from the space of being present. In terms of money, the larger the amount of money that flows to the poor apart from a relationship, the more likely the givers are supporting systems that caused the injustice in the first place. Our monetary help thereby often works to further prop up the power of the evil structures, the very same structures that produce and reproduce the cycles of poverty in the first place.

In various places in the New Testament (2 Cor 8:4; Phil 1:5, 7) the apostle Paul talks of sharing financially in one another's burdens as being a fellowship, a deep communion or, in my words, a kinship. In Philippians 4:14-15 Paul associates sharing financially in someone's burdens as sharing in their sufferings as well. This all testifies to the ways giving and economy are not offered by

Christians to the poor in a detached mode of assistance. They are part of a kinship we already share with one another.

A church in the Toronto suburbs decided to do a care ministry *for* the poor in an impoverished urban section of the city. They drove several miles every Sunday afternoon, bringing food and clothing from their church. They would arrive at the building, set up the clothing to distribute, and warm the food to be served. They would set up tables and arrange the food on them. They would read a Scripture, give thanks, and say a blessing over the food. Then they would set up the food line. Those from the suburban church would serve on one side of the table, and the homeless and needy would line up on the other side to receive the food. The suburbanites would try to talk with those who were homeless or struggling. After a few hours, they would clean up and depart in time to get home, relax with their families, and prepare for the upcoming week.

This went on for months until one Sunday afternoon a few people started to evaluate what was happening at this soup kitchen. They asked the recipients of the ministry what they liked about the program. Were the food or clothes enough? What would they change if they could? Surprisingly, the homeless and hurting said things like, "We'd like to bring food too. We have food stamps, we have gift cards, and we'd like to bring food and share it as well. We'd like to help clean up too. We'd like to serve you sometimes."

Stunned and surprised, these people from the suburbs changed their approach to the food pantry ministry. They asked the homeless and poor if they could fellowship with them. The homeless and poor helped set up the tables the way they preferred. Those without homes and the poor now served those from the suburbs, and they shared tables together. The ensuing dynamic reshaped everything that went on between the people. Soon, such deep relationships started to develop, that some twenty or so people moved to this deeply distressed neighborhood. A few short years later a church grew up in this place. People's lives on all sides of the tables were changed. Kingdom broke out.[1]

It is only through being present to the other, what I have called kinship, that God changes the world. In this relational space with the marginalized and hurting, God's authority and presence in Jesus Christ becomes real and can be tended to. Here an economy takes shape where each one's life has purpose, meaning, and a role to play. Here economic resources can be shared as family. Goods are shared out of an abundance from God, not as a charitable gift from one who has to the one who has not.

For all these reasons, people of privilege, people of means, people who have never suffered the brutalities of life must submit to the practice of being with those who have. When we do this, a space is opened up that is beyond our own control. We encounter God in Christ in the flesh. In the process we see our own deficits, the ways we have never depended on God, the ways we have kept in control. A new world is born: the kingdom of God.

THE REAL PRESENCE OF CHRIST
AND HIS KINGDOM

Remember once more the parable of the final judgment in Matthew 25. Jesus tells his disciples in essence that he is present among them when they are with the "least of these." Using similar words elsewhere, Jesus says, "Whoever welcomes one such child in my name welcomes me" (Mt 18:5) and "Whoever listens to you listens to me" (Lk 10:16). As in these other places Jesus makes it clear: his real presence is sacramentally located in the practice of being with the poor.

We should expect the dynamics of Christ's reign to take shape in the space we inhabit with the poor. As we are present, we become like kin. We share what we have as we would with any friend. Yet we never take on the role of caretaker or superior. Instead a new socioeconomics takes shape among us that is beyond the haves and the have-nots. We pray for healing and anoint as the Spirit moves. We proclaim the gospel. We share struggles and receive prayer. We share our financial resources. In so doing, resources are not expended but multiplied. There is a relational reordering of our lives in this new, wonderful, surprising space. The kingdom of God is being made visible. And a whole new world is born. It is the world of faithful presence.

While I sat in McDonald's studying, my friend Wayne came over and sat in my booth. The right side of his jaw was swollen twice the size of the other side. I could tell one of his teeth was impacted and infection had set in. He was in great pain. I had known Wayne for two years. He'd been without a home this whole time and was living in his van. I looked at him, and in my own human frailty worried how much this extraordinary dental work was going to cost me. Nevertheless, the Holy Spirit pushed, and soon thereafter I wrote the phone number of my dentist on a napkin. I asked Wayne to make an appointment, and if the dentist asked who would pay, Wayne was to have him call me and I would guarantee payment. Secretively, I thought my church would pay. (We had a large mission fund to help defray costs of people in mission.) The next day the dentist called, and I promised to cover all costs. I said I would do it for any friend in need like that. Wayne's teeth were treated and healed. Many weeks passed, and I waited for a bill, which never came. The dentist decided not to bill Wayne. Two months later, as Wayne and I were talking, Wayne thanked me again for paying for his dental work. I said, "Wayne, I never got a bill." Wayne was shocked. I said, "Wayne, I literally did nothing. God used me to facilitate the kingdom. What you experienced was the kingdom."

British Anglican priest and theologian Sam Wells lived among one of the poorer sections of London. He once wrote these words:

> Poverty is not primarily about money. It is about having no idea what to do and/or having no one with whom to do it. The former I called imagination and the latter I called community. To the extent that our neighborhood had imagination and community, we were not poor. But without imagination and community, no money could help us. . . . The role of the local church is to be a *community of imagination* [for the kingdom].[2]

These words speak to a reality I have witnessed time and again as I have practiced the discipline of being with the "least of these."

BEING WITH THE "LEAST OF THESE"
IN ALL THREE CIRCLES

The book of Acts describes the local church being present to the poor in their own close circles. Acts 4:34-35, for example, reads, "There was not a needy person among them, for as many as owned lands or houses sold them and brought the proceeds of what was sold. They laid it at the apostles' feet, and it was distributed to each as any had need." It is evident from this text how much the first Christians knew each other's needs. They gave as an act of submission and worship ("laid it at the apostles' feet"). We know that the first churches in Acts organized deacons to care for the widows among them. The whole community was pleased with this decision (Acts 6:5). Being *with* the needy started in the close circle of fellowship. Here, being aware and present to the hurting shaped the imagination and drove the way they organized their common way of life.

The apostle Paul, likewise, organized the offerings from the Gentile churches to relieve the suffering among the needy of the Jerusalem church. In

Galatians 2, Paul recounts how he and Barnabas were commissioned as apostles in their visit to Jerusalem. He then reports that "they asked only one thing, that we remember the poor, which was actually what I was eager to do" (Gal 2:10). The early church, then, practiced "remembering" the poor much like they "remembered" Christ at the Table: being present to the poor. It was a principle fundamental to their life together.

Being with the "least of these" must begin with the close circle. Here, Jesus is the host. Here, Christians learn to discern Christ's real presence among the poor, first by tending to his presence among the poor who are already part of the body. When the apostle Paul urges the Christians to "work for the good of all," but do it "especially for those of the family of faith" (Gal 6:10), he is giving a gentle nod to the priority of the close circle. Being with the "least of these" must therefore become part of every new believer's discipleship. It must become a way of life. And from here it can be practiced in the neighborhoods, the other two circles of life.

The early church followed the life and example of Jesus in the dotted and half circles of their lives. As Jesus walked the towns and villages of Galilee and Judea, he spent time with people, eating with them at their tables, being present in their neighborhoods, proclaiming the gospel—the coming of the kingdom. His very presence would gather people around him. Spaces would open up. Where there was faith, trust, and submission to him, miracles occurred. Where there was no faith, he could do no miracles (Mt 13:58; Mk 6:5). Faith in him was most often found among the sick, the hurting, the outcasts, and those who were despised. There, people were healed, sins forgiven, new life began. This is the way the New Testament church understood the meaning of being with the poor. This is the way they lived in the neighborhoods.

The early church of the first four centuries lived the practice of being with the "least of these" in all three circles of their lives.

RECOVERING FAITHFUL PRESENCE
AMONG THE "LEAST OF THESE"

Even a casual review of church history reveals how the church, once known for seeing Jesus' healing presence at work among the sick, had moved the practice of being with the "least of these" to a maintenance function of the church. By the thirteenth century, for instance, the sacrament of anointing the sick, once called unction, had become extreme unction—preparing people for their death.

In the words of Catholic historian A. M. Henry, the church had forgotten the sacrament's "power to deliver from bodily ailments."[3]

As with all the other practices, once the church becomes comfortable in Christendom, it naturally organizes its functions to take care of Christians. The church took healing from the streets and made anointing with oil an officially sanctioned sacrament available on request. There was now less focus on encountering Christ in the sick, the hurting, and the poor in the streets. The church instead focused on meting out the comforts of forgiveness, absolution, and dying in the peace of Christ to Christians. The encounter with the unpredictable presence of God among the "least of these" was lost. The church had drifted into maintenance mode.

When parts of the Reformation rejected Christ's presence at the mass, they also rejected his presence among the poor. Almsgiving was turned into a civic program in many parts of the Reformation. Much mercy was accomplished. Unfortunately, the loss of Christ's real presence *with* the poor profoundly changed the practice of being with the "least of these." It turned it into a maintenance program.

Today, most churches do similar things. We turn being with the poor into a justice program that Christians can volunteer for by signing up for a few hours a month. We build justice centers on our church campuses and require the poor to come to us. We separate ourselves from being with the least of these. And the mission of God is thwarted.

In worship, Christians rarely know that someone sitting next to them is struggling with poverty. Our financial and personal struggles remain hidden because we are too ashamed to talk about them in a church where everyone shows only their Sunday best. We know how to engage the poor only through a justice program. So we ignore the poor among us and rush to start justice programs with the poor in our neighborhoods. But we do not practice being with the poor. As a result we miss the direct encounter with the living Christ in our midst and in our neighborhoods. In the process we risk our own damnation, not even knowing it (Mt 25:41).

We must therefore lead in a different way. We must lead our churches to a new experience of Christ's presence among the poor and the most vulnerable. We start with a posture of *withness*, in the close circle. We learn how to be present with those who hurt. We gather as kin. Once we have learned to do this, we are better trained as a people to be present to the poor in the other circles of our lives. We then ask every Christian to spend regular time in hospitals, prisons, half-way houses, and homeless shelters to be present to the already faithful presence of Christ. Here, the fields are ripe for harvest, ready for outbreaks of healing miracles among the poor, sick, and hurting. This is the way God changes the world.

FIVE

BEING WITH CHILDREN

Every Saturday morning my ten-year-old son and I sit across from one another in a local greasy spoon eating breakfast. I direct my attention to his face. He struggles to sit still. He can barely stand it. He wants to play a video game on my phone or read a Calvin and Hobbes comic book. I quietly say no thanks and ask him for three topics. It's all part of the Saturday-morning ritual we've been doing for years. Nonetheless, he still grimaces and lets go an exasperating "Oh, Dad." He chooses two topics. I choose one. He says,

"Dogs, airplanes," and I say, "School, let's talk about the highlights and lowlights of school this week." "Oh, Dad." And slowly, we begin the exchange. So much more important than anything I say, or he says, is my posture at the table. I sit peacefully. I cast my eyes on him and give him the entire focus of my face. I am intentionally trusting that Jesus will be present in this space we inhabit together, and I am tending to what God by his Spirit is doing among us. Nothing affects my child more than when I take time to sit with him across a table and tend to Christ's presence.

Our children are the casualties of a crazy, confusing, frenzied society. The world can't be trusted, they are told. We therefore need certified programs for everything. Sports, music, tutoring, dancing, the arts, Boy Scouts, Girl Scouts, and gaming must all be programmed, and leaders must be screened for past crimes and sexual history. As the children shuffle from one scrubbed program to another, their souls are pushed and pulled, looking for the right path to direct their passions. They are waiting to be drawn in to a place worthy of their trust. They are longing to know and be known. Children yearn for face-to-face presence.

BEING WITH CHILDREN

Historically, the practice of guiding children has been a central fact of life in the church. Even today, when new congregations form in North America, one of the first tasks the leaders pay heed to is teaching and guiding children, which is often called "children's ministries."

To this day the practice of tending to children defines a people as coming together to be a church. Through various means, churches pass on the story of God in Jesus Christ to our children. We have ways of grafting parents, godparents, and communities into supportive communal practices that, together as part of regular family life, allow us to pray, teach, read, and direct the young child's life. We have ways of initiating children into adulthood. All of these practices are inseparable from what it means to be the church. What we often miss, however, is the reality that Jesus becomes present in these spaces. As the adult becomes present to the child, the space between them becomes the place of faithful presence.

THE KINGDOM VALUE OF WELCOMING CHILDREN

Matthew 18 opens with the disciples jockeying for position again. They ask Jesus who among them will get the best post with the most power in the kingdom to come. Jesus points to a child and says this is the way the kingdom will work: unless you change and become like this child, you won't make it into the kingdom. Children, those with no status in this ancient world, will be the ones who have status in the kingdom. Then he says the all-important words: "Whoever welcomes one such child in my name welcomes me" (v. 5). He uses the important word *welcome*, which connotes patience, embrace, openness, and genuineness. It communicates the posture of receiving someone into my presence. Jesus says, when you do this with a child, you enter the very kingdom of God (v. 3). When you receive a child into your presence, you also receive the presence of Jesus. A space is opened up where God can work. It is a space where God in Christ not only transforms children's lives but the adults in the space as well.

Very early on in the beginning of the Life on the Vine Christian Community, we decided to resist making children's ministries into a program. We wanted to lead the community into being *with* our children. From the very beginning, we asked every member to spend time with the children during a Bible story time. At various times we would say that by being with the children, you were being prepared to experience the kingdom. If you refused, you might be refusing the kingdom itself.

When our congregation grew, we decided to have our children with us for as much as possible in the main worship gathering. They were with us for the stories of wonder, a time of telling what God had been doing in our lives during the week. This opened the beginning of our gathering.

As we bowed in silence, sometimes for as long as ten minutes, they would be with us. The children found silence strangely interesting. They were with us for the invocation, the call to worship, and the reading of Scripture, and then, right before the sermon, we dismissed them for their own time of hearing the story told and the Word proclaimed over their lives. We asked the appropriate age groups to head toward the doors, and as they did we raised our hands toward them and blessed them, saying, "The Lord be with you as you worship." The children responded, "and also with you." They returned after the sermon to gather with us again and be blessed around the table, sing praises to God, and receive the benediction. The time when the children left for their own storytelling time was a special time with the children. We adopted storytelling methods based on the curriculum called "Godly Play."[1] We emphasized adults getting on the level of the child, inviting God's presence by the Spirit to be with us, then telling the story slowly, allowing space for wondering and questions, and above all being present to God. Adults spent time being with the children as they explored. This space between the adult and the child became sacred.

We asked everyone in the church to participate in this ministry with children. There were regular teachers rotating in and out, but everyone was asked to participate. All adults were asked to be in the children's ministry a minimum of once every eight weeks. They were asked to be present with our children, to know them, to be changed by them. This resulted in a community where our children could grow up recognizing Jesus not purely as a historical person and a doctrine, but as someone present to us in our daily lives. We recognized, in this screen-crazy society, the space for his presence would never be more available with our children than during these early years.

It was difficult to convey to our church community that Jesus was actually present in this space with our children. One time a member of our church community who contributed in so many ways to the life of the church approached me and said that he wished to be excused from children's ministry. Doug said to me that "working with children is not

my gift." I responded, "Being with children in our
teaching ministry is not a spiritual gift. It is never
mentioned in the Scripture as a spiritual gift. Instead, the church brings all its gifts to the space
of ministry with children. And all who can lower
themselves to be present with a child will experience Jesus and his kingdom like nowhere else."
Several years later, Doug looked back at his experience at Life on the Vine and told me that he
experienced the renewal in his life with Christ first
and foremost in his blossoming relationship
with children.

THE PRESENCE OF CHRIST WITH CHILDREN

Paul exhorts children to "obey your parents in the
Lord, for this is right. 'Honor your father and
mother'" (Eph 6:1-2). Then, immediately following,
he exhorts fathers not to provoke children to anger
but serve them by bringing them up in "the discipline and instruction of the Lord" (v. 4). Scholars
have shown how revolutionary these words were
in their first-century context. In a day when
children were viewed as inferior and patriarchs
ruled with an iron fist, Paul, contrary to the pre-
vailing culture, calls parent and child into a space
of mutuality in the Lord. The parent is not singularly over the child. The child is considered too.

Parent and child come together under the one Lord in a mutuality between them that honors their respective roles. This text falls under the opening text of the Household Codes (Eph 5:20–6:9), where Paul says, "Submit to one another out of reverence for Christ" (Eph 5:21 NIV). And so the apostle is describing a revolutionary relationship of presence between adult and child under the Lord's reign.

This speaks once again to the way the practices make space for Jesus' presence as each person submits to him as Lord. Children are asked to obey their parents *in the Lord*, and the parents are asked to serve their children *in the Lord*. Parents play their role yet release control. Jesus is the one who works in this relationship.

Just as it is in the practice of reconciliation, "in my name" is used here as well. As with reconciliation, "in my name" marks off the space that gathers people into Jesus' presence under his authority as Lord and King. In this space the dynamic of Ephesians 6:1-2 is rehearsed. And so Jesus promises to be especially present here with children just as he does in reconciliation (Mt 18:20).

The stunning reality is that being with children is an encounter with the living Christ. Just as with our gathering around the table, so likewise here we gather around children. We set aside our striving and quiet our need to control. We enter their space and tend to their presence. In their vulnerabilities, my own vulnerabilities are exposed. In so doing, a space is opened up, and Jesus becomes present and begins to work. As a result, the space for direction and care is opened up for his kingdom.

It is not surprising then that the church has viewed the process of initiating children as sacramental. But what we see now, in light of Matthew 18:1-5, is that being *with* children is the process whereby we become present to children and together present to Christ as part of everyday life. The sacrament of being with children is a social sacrament that brings together the community in its *withness* with the child. This is what we have lost. This is what we must recover for the mission of God in the world.

Because children are not yet jaded, they can often more easily be open to Christ's presence. So at Life on the Vine we discovered that children sometimes led the adults into tending to Christ's presence. Thus, learning went way beyond the rote memorizing of doctrine or Scripture, beyond the cognitive lessons or even storytelling. Together children and adults learned to tend to Christ's presence in their lives.

WHERE THE KINGDOM TAKES PLACE

As the Matthew 18 episode begins, the disciples wonder who among them will get the positions of authority in the new kingdom. How will life be ordered in the kingdom, and who will have power over others? Jesus, just as he did around the table in Luke 22, must reorient their understanding of how the kingdom of God works. This time he orients them around a child.

He calls a child and "placed the child among them" (Mt 18:2 NIV). The text emphasizes the space Jesus opens up among them around the child. He then says that unless you change and become like this child, "you will never enter the kingdom of heaven" (v. 3). This is the space of the kingdom. The one who becomes humble like this child enters the authority of the kingdom (v. 4).

There is more going on here than Jesus merely using the child's humble posture as a metaphor for what is necessary to enter the kingdom (although it is that). Jesus is saying that in entering the space of the child, his presence is here, and to the extent one can submit to his presence, as this child did, a reorientation of the world will begin. Here, in this space of the child, the kingdom will take shape.

The stakes are high. In Matthew 18:6-7 Jesus says, "If any of you put a stumbling block before one of these little ones who believe in me, it would be better for you if a great millstone were fastened around your neck and you were drowned in the depth of the sea. Woe to the world because of stumbling blocks!" This statement reminds us that in his presence heaven and earth are moved, just as they are in the practice of reconciliation (Mt 18:18-19). The only other place Jesus shows anger beside the clearing of the temple is when the disciples speak sternly to the children, keeping them from Jesus (Mk 10:14). Critical things are at stake in the spaces we open to be present with our children. And we must tend to these spaces and discern them carefully.

It's important to tend not only to the child's presence but to Christ in the midst of this sacred space. Both being present to children and tending to Christ's presence becomes real in the space between us and children. In all the practices, we have become used to this pattern of faithful presence.

Parents therefore must invite children to tend to the presence of Christ as we worship, as we share the table. First be with them, and then guide their (and your) sight to the presence of Christ among us. In this space God will do great things.

I have now been sitting in worship with my
ten-year-old son for years. It has always been a
twofold struggle to tend to him first and then,
together with him, to the presence of Christ. Like
many parents I have often been tempted to allow
my son to become the center of my attention, especially during his younger years. During worship I
discovered the more I centered my attention on
him, the more others' attention would be drawn
to him. So I encouraged him: "Can you give your
attention to God? Can you give thanks to God with
your singing? Can you use your music to give God
praise for all he's done for us? Can you sense God's
presence in the room this morning?" At night
before bed, after reading either the Bible or another
story, before we'd pray, I'd ask, "Can you sense
God's presence here in the room with us?" Around
the dinner table together we would pray for sen-
sitivity to God's presence among us. I learned to
both model my own tending as well as direct his
tending to the presence of God in Christ. This kind
of direction can only happen after I myself have
established being present to my son.

We must constantly balance between being
present to our children and directing their gaze
and ours jointly to the presence of Christ. Loving
our children in this way is so important. By together

tending to Jesus in the space between us, we avoid idolizing our children. There are times when admiring our children affirms them and gives them rightful confidence. But we must resist centering our lives around our children and instead center our lives together with them in Christ's presence.

BEING WITH CHILDREN
IN ALL THREE CIRCLES

Most churches think of children's ministry as a church program, particularly on Sunday mornings. With few exceptions, children's ministry takes place in and around the church building. The practice of being with children, however, moves children's ministries into our everyday lives. It disciplines us to be with children in all three circles as an entire way of life.

Being with children most often begins in the close circles of life because it takes Christians to practice it. We discern Christ's presence with children just as we do around the Lord's Table. In the circle of Christians we have the confidence to believe that Christ's presence will come to be with us and our children. As Christians, we can navigate the tension between being present to our children and guiding our attention jointly to his presence. If we can do this in the close circle, we will be able to do the same in the other equally important circles of life.

Of course, being with children must move beyond the close circle. It must become part of our everyday lives. The place of presence between adult and child must become the trusted place our children know they can go any time they have questions during the week, struggling with beliefs, doubts, and the confusions of our day. Here they can find guidance via the trust built up in the real presence of Christ. Here they can safely go to be heard. Here they can seriously discern the goodness of God and come to know Christ's presence and rule over all evil. Here, every day, they will grow into their identities in Christ. As we practice this discipline together in our families, our neighborhood house gatherings, or wherever we hang out with children, neighbors can look on and see the kingdom. The dotted circles of our lives provide the theater for our neighbors and friends to understand the way the kingdom works through our children.

This then also means that being with children must move into all the half circles of our lives as well. Far from children being a hindrance to mission in our neighborhoods, being with children is actually an important way we discern and give witness to God's kingdom coming in the world.

I have often heard parents of little children say they are too busy for mission. When our child, Max, came into our lives, I remember my wife and I going through adjustments. Rae Ann (my wife) was used to going to work every day, being with people, being out with friends. Now she was a stay-at-home mom. Out of her need, she reached out. She started getting together with other moms who were going through similar adjustments. Out of mutual need, my wife was meeting more people outside the faith than I ever could have. Moms groups were popping up all over the place. She got to know many women struggling with raising children and with marriage itself. To this day, Max has been one of the best means to connect us to hurting people. When I and other dads were invited to the get-togethers, we would sit together stunned at the community these women shared. As my wife and I tended to Max, we would tend to other children. Connections were made. We met people of all faiths, and atheists as well. Max opened up a world where witness to the kingdom could happen naturally and unimposed.

I have seen parents entering worlds where people are paranoid of other adults being with their children. We as Christians must therefore come into these spaces on invitation only. This may take shape as we are invited to other people's homes for play dates, for moms (or parents) groups, or neighborhood birthday parties. We may volunteer for cafeteria duty at the local elementary school. We may become tutors at the local schools. As we enter, we come to be with children. We are present to children as we tend to the presence of Jesus working among them. Children are transformed by love and presence. As strangers take notice, spaces are opened for healing the abuses and pains of families. Here, in these half circles of our lives, being with children becomes another mode of the church's faithful presence in the world.

This kind of presence with children should lead Christians to be the leaders in adopting and foster-parenting children into our families. As adoption becomes more difficult, more costly, and more regulated by misconceived motivations and agendas, Christians can establish homes for adoption that give witness to another way. We can come alongside pregnant women who have no family support and care for them, their new babies, and their future. We can help women see that their children are loved by God and that he has a plan for them far beyond what they can think or imagine. The many crisis pregnancy centers and adoption agencies cared for already by Christians bears witness to the presence of Christ with children. These are some of the half circles of our lives where God is calling us to be present to children.

RECOVERING FAITHFUL PRESENCE AMONG CHILDREN

In its first three hundred years the early church was renowned for being with children in the streets. Across the Greco-Roman world, Christians took children off the streets where they had been left to die. They adopted children into their homes and cared for them. The early church's convictions about children led to their singular stand against the common practices of infanticide and abortion in their day. This stunning witness of the early church can be directly tied to its practices of being with children in and among the neighborhoods.

And yet the church has regularly defaulted to maintenance mode when it comes to caring for children. With the official sponsoring of Christianity by Rome via Constantine, there were now crushing numbers of infant baptisms coming into the church. The bishops could not get to all the baptisms, so confirmations now (following the baptisms) had to be delayed. Slowly confirmation became a regimented process enforced over the

Roman church. We can see in this history the struggle of the church to maintain the presence of Jesus in the practice of being with children. We can see the tendency to take the practice of being with children out of the neighborhoods and put it under the sanctioning presence of a professional. Our churches must work hard to resist taking the practice of being with children out of everyday life.

We must resist defaulting to maintenance modes of church where we seek to keep busy Christian parents happy and coming back to church. We must work hard against extracting children out of worship and out of our lives in order to control their behavior. We must make space for adults to be with children and for them to be with us in worship. Then from here, once the presence of Christ is truly experienced and we've learned how to tend to his presence among our children, we can enter the other circles of our lives with our children. We can be faithfully present to Christ's presence among the children of the world.

SIX

THE FIVEFOLD GIFTING

Nobody loves a bully. This is true even in American business. Yet we don't know how else to lead except by position over someone. As a community of people, we want accountability, we need authority, and yet we desire mutuality. But we don't know how that is possible.

Most North Americans have experienced managerial coercion at one time or another. It could be a boss threatening our paycheck if we don't do something, an expert consultant evaluating our work in a heavy-handed manner, or a police officer stopping us and issuing a ticket for a debatable infraction. It could be something much worse: racial profiling, violent threats, vicious accusations. To some degree, these are common to everyday life. The world runs on coercion. Despite our best intentions, as courteous as everyone tries to be, when all else fails we default to negotiation by position. The threats are subtle. The use of influence and position is indirect. You over me, me over you; you against me, me against you.

Churches in North America, it appears, have taken on these bad habits. In Seattle, Minneapolis, and other places, several high visibility pastors have been forced to resign or take a leave of absence of their own volition. These did not occur because of a sexual failure or financial impropriety, but because of abusive behavior toward people working under them. In the years 2014 and 2015, Internet conversations arose concerning the prevalence of narcissistic personality disorder among senior pastors of large churches. Christians are increasingly wary of pastors' abusive leadership practices when they appear to be imposing their will on a congregation.

Nonetheless, hierarchy still dominates Christian thinking about leadership. Despite the new popularity of participant management styles in the business world, despite the rise of agile software development bringing people together to develop collaborative work environments, most Protestant churches are still led by a senior pastor or lead pastor at the top of the organizational chain. So, whenever I speak in church settings about multiple leadership, about having no senior pastor, about being led by several leaders operating together as a group, people push back: "How will anything ever get done this way? We need a leader at the top, where the buck stops." Like the nation of Israel in 1 Samuel 8:6, we shout our pleas to God: "Give us a king!" We need someone at the top who we can all look to and understand where this place is going.

No group of people can exist for long without authority functioning well in leadership. And so the world accepts, and the church defaults to, hierarchical systems. We work and organize beneath the heavy hand that governs us. But we long for something more. The world may operate on coercion, but it aches for mutuality.

THE PRACTICE OF THE FIVEFOLD GIFTING

As Jesus and the disciples headed into Jerusalem on Jesus' last, fateful trip, the disciples once again started clamoring for their place at the top of the pecking order in the coming new kingdom. James and John asked to sit at Jesus' right and left side in the kingdom. They were saying, "Put us in the best position to be over the people." Upon hearing this, the rest of the disciples were indignant. Jesus calmed them down and replied,

> You know that among the Gentiles those whom they recognize as their rulers lord it over them, and their great ones are tyrants over them. But it is not so among you; but whoever wishes to become great among you must be your servant, and whoever wishes to be first among you must be slave of all. (Mk 10:42-44)

For Jesus, authority in the kingdom would be exercised in no other way. There would be no hierarchy, no coercive power, no one person ruling over and above another person. His model is mutual, shared leadership under one Lord.

But how can this be? How would this actually work in the community of the new kingdom? How could a people of God function without hierarchy? The answer is the practice of the fivefold ministry. The answer is recognizing those among us who are gifted by the Holy Spirit to lead in their respective giftings and enabling them to exercise those gifts in mutual submission to one another.

The clearest outline of the fivefold gifting is laid out in Ephesians 4. The chapter starts with Paul challenging the Ephesians "to lead a life worthy of the calling to which you have been called" (v. 1). Paul is not speaking to individuals here. He is picturing a group of people brought together under the mutual worship of one Lord. They were to lead a worthy life together in "humility and gentleness, with patience, bearing with one another with love" (v. 2). There will be conflict, for sure. But in these conflicts, we will make "every effort to maintain the unity of the Spirit in the bond of peace" (v. 3). Because through one baptism we all participate in "one Lord, . . . one God and Father of all" (vv. 5-6). This is a picture of a people gathered under the authority of one Lord, working it out mutually.

Quoting from Psalm 68, Paul pictures Jesus as enthroned at the place of ultimate authority, the right hand of the Father. From this place of his ascension "he gave gifts to his people" (Eph 4:8). Paul then recites the five gifts: "Some would be apostles, some prophets, some evangelists, some pastors and teachers." They are given "to equip the saints for the work of ministry, for building up the body of Christ" (vv. 11-12). The five gifts are given directly from the Lord in power. The gifted people are to lead in dependence on that same Lord. And yet all this takes place within a community of mutual participation in this trust and authority.

There isn't space here to provide an extensive description of each of the five gifts. Suffice it to say that (1) *apostles* initiate, gather, and pioneer new works, calling people to live now in the kingdom; (2) *prophets* speak so as to reveal the truth and call of God into a situation, especially the injustice and neglect of the poor; (3) *pastors* tend to and sustain people's souls, especially the hurting; (4) *evangelists* bring the good news to those who are hurting; and (5) *teachers* help explain and deepen people's faith. Let's focus most immediately on how the fivefold gifting functions as a discipline that opens space for the presence of Christ among us. This space becomes the place of his authority and direction for the community into mission.

THE MUTUALITY AND INTERDEPENDENCE OF THE LEADERSHIP

The gifts in Ephesians 4:8-12 are multiple and interdependent. No one person can carry out all the gifts in the community. Each person is to stay within the boundaries of their own giftedness as "according to the measure of Christ's gift" (v. 7). Elsewhere, the apostle Paul makes explicit that "to each is given the manifestation of the Spirit for the common good" (1 Cor 12:7). The Spirit allots these gifts to each person "individually just as the Spirit chooses" (1 Cor 12:11). No one can say to another, we have no need of your gift (1 Cor 12:21). The gifts cannot function on their own. We are all inextricably related to one another and must always lead within our respective gift in mutual submission to one another. It appears then that these gifts open up a space socially where people become interdependent, and the Holy Spirit works in that interdependence. Opposed to the striving, competition, and violence of the world, this community is formed by the opposite, the mutual participation in the presence of Christ.

The gifted leaders, together in mutual submission to each other's gifts, discern the mind of Christ for each situation (1 Cor 2:14-16). This is collaborative leadership. This was the way God worked through history through the nation of Israel.

When Life on the Vine was starting, I took whatever support funds we had for the first few years and distributed them among multiple leaders.

I kept my marketplace job, and instead of using all of the funds for my own support I redirected those funds to help people free up time for ministry. These funds, not even enough to support one pastor, were split between four pastors. I would say, "I see you excelling at doing this work in our community. Do you see the same? If we could find $1,000 a month to help you, could you free up ten to fifteen hours a week to give to the shaping of our church with your ministry?"

As a group of leaders, we worked through a gift inventory from time to time. This was a quick multiple-choice type test that could be taken and scored in fifteen minutes. We each got an assessment of our strengths and weaknesses among the five giftings.[1] It was irrelevant whether the test was accurate, because the object of the exercise was to discuss the results of the test for each person. We would ask each other questions such as, Have we all experienced this person's strengths and weak-nesses in the same way as the test did? How have you experienced this person's gifts? What emerges is an idea of what each person's giftings are (there can be more than one) and what strengths and weaknesses each person possesses. Recognizing our weaknesses makes us more readily dependent on everyone else. Our job descriptions were refined each time, and a wonderful mutuality developed out of this process. We learned how to trust and challenge each other in the joint leadership of the community.

We expect each leader to lead within the domain of their recognized gift. As an issue arises in the community, the leaders meet to discern it. Each leader gives their opinion from within their own gifting. Sometimes leaders assume that all we need is conversation in order for things to get sorted out. But I learned along the way to encourage the one bringing the issue to the table to make a proposal. If the evangelist brings up an urgent need in the neighborhood, I ask the person, "Do you have a proposal?" This usually is enough for us to get going. Then it's up to the evangelistic leader to submit a proposal to the group. We don't take a vote. We discuss it out of our giftings. The pastor speaks to the needs of the individuals involved and how they will be affected by such a proposal. The apostle speaks to the proposal's urgency, and so on. Gradually the proposal takes a deeper shape, and we become of one mind. Sometimes the proposal is ditched entirely for something else. If everyone agrees, or those who disagree only disagree on a minor issue, we present the proposal to the whole church. The leadership group is a pneumatocracy (governed by the Spirit). Each person must lead out of their gifting and submit their proposals to the rest of the body for further development and eventual mutual assent.

In meetings like this, I have become deeply aware of my need for my friends' giftings that are different from mine. I, as an apostle, can be overzealous, quick to move, and may not take into account the effect my proposals might have on the souls of people. I need to listen with special care to the pastors in our midst who so often speak in ways that challenge me. I must trust this space between us where Jesus has come to dwell. I must submit myself to his presence at work in this holy space of his gifts. By so doing, every decision that comes forth becomes a communal decision that moves us deep into the center of his will and his mind. This space becomes the center of his faithful presence.

THE PRIORITY OF
THE FIRST LEADER GROUP

In Ephesians 4:12 Paul says the gifts are for the equipping of "the saints for the work of ministry, for building up the body of Christ." The fivefold gifts appear to be given priority in the ministry of the whole body. Yet this does not diminish the fact that the entire church is in ministry. The purpose of these five gifts is to "equip" the rest of the church for ministry. Establishing this group of gifts sets the rest of the gifts into motion in the body as a whole. This is why Paul says to the Corinthians, who are overfocusing on the sensational gifts, especially the gift of tongues, that they should together "strive for the greater gifts" (1 Cor 12:31). They should locate and recognize the first gifts, which set the rest in motion and guide the other gifts into their rightful order.

When planting a church I have noticed that when the leadership is functioning well, the rest of the church community becomes a fully gifted community empowered for mission. When the first five leaders are functioning well as a team, they know how to recognize the gifts in others in the wider community. They model mutual submission before the community. They are used to recognizing the gifts and boundaries in each other, and so they now go, recognize, and affirm the gifts in the rest of the community. They mobilize the power of the kingdom.

At Life on the Vine we believed our denomination's ordination process worked well to facilitate the ordering of the first gifts. It served as a starting point to initiate a group of leaders for a community. It provided the testing grounds for the fitness and commitment of these leaders. But this doesn't mean these leaders are now over the others in the community. Each leader serves under the community, not over it. Each leader's gifts still had to be recognized within the community (or there would be no community).

In summary, recognizing the fivefold ministry is the first order of every community. But they too must then release the rest of the community's giftedness or all will be lost. This founding group of leaders sets the blueprint for the rest of the church's leadership culture. But they are never to be above the other gifted leaders. Everyone operates in mutual submission to one another and to the whole congregation. As the fivefold ministers are present to one another, they in turn become present to Christ at work among the community. They themselves become a model of practicing faithful presence.

EXERCISING AUTHORITY
IN CHRIST'S PRESENCE

It is stunning to realize that the authority and power of the risen King comes to reside among men and women in the gifts of his people (Eph 4:7). But lest anyone think they can gain control of this authority, as soon as they seek to control or manipulate the authority of the King, his authority and presence depart. Gifted leaders therefore must always exercise their gifts in total trust and dependence on the Lord.

Paul says the goal of the gifts functioning together is to "come to the unity of the faith and of the knowledge of the Son of God, to complete maturity, to the measure of the fullness of Christ" (Eph 4:13, my translation). This is where the gifts together lead the community. The word Paul uses for fullness overlaps in meaning with the *Shekinah* presence of God in the Jewish temple. It is a word peculiarly chosen by the apostle to refer to Christ's "full and real presence" in his body, the church. For Paul, ultimately, this is the goal of mutually submitting to one another's gifts—his presence.

When Christian leaders are present to each other and present to Christ's presence working among them, they experience the fullness of his presence. Likewise, when all gifts are functioning, they lead the rest of the church to be similarly present to each other and Christ's presence. Paul likens the result to the *Shekinah* presence of Christ dwelling among us. The practice of the fivefold ministry is the basis for leading a church to be faithfully present to Christ in the world.

THE FIVEFOLD GIFTING
IN THE THREE CIRCLES

Given what we've examined so far, it is obvious the formation of the fivefold gifting starts in a close circle, in the space of mutual submission to Jesus Christ as Lord. Because these leadership gifts are an extension of Christ's lordship, they are impossible apart from discerning our submission to his reign and presence by the Holy Spirit.

But it is a fallacy to think that the fivefold ministries are only for leading within the church's close circle. We already know that once they are set in place, they help recognize and facilitate all the other gifts in the close circle. But they also do the same in the dotted circles and half circles of our lives.

Nowhere is the fivefold ministry needed more than in our neighborhoods. Indeed, it's hard to imagine how the dotted circle fellowships could be possible apart from the fivefold ministries. For instance, the house gathering in the neighborhood that gathers weekly to share a meal requires an initiator to gather people together and commit regularly for a meal. This initiator will most likely be an apostle. When a church seeks to develop house fellowships in the neighborhoods, it should probably start with locating the apostles in our midst.

Likewise, there will be times when an evangelist is needed in the house gathering. As we gather in homes in each neighborhood, an evangelistically gifted person will need to be present, calling attention to needs in the neighborhood and then to lead engagements in response. Pastors will also be needed to respond to the soul care needs of everyday life. The entire fivefold ministry is needed in every neighborhood, which in turn mobilizes all of the gifts among us. This is essential for the kingdom of God to break out in our neighborhoods. Thus every dotted circle in the neighborhood should locate the apostles, prophets, teachers, evangelists, and pastors in their midst.

In my travels I often encounter churches struggling to form missional communities in neighborhoods. My first question is whether they know who the apostles are in the neighborhoods and what have they done to locate, affirm, train, and send them out. Of course, these apostles eventually need around them pastors and teachers and the other gifts. But apostles most often are the ones who get things started.

The practice of locating, recognizing, and submitting to the fivefold ministry will push ministry into the half circles of our lives as well. From their location in the dotted circles, these leaders will inhabit places where there is great need. The apostle will mobilize prayer and resources where needed. The evangelist will tend to the gospel. Where someone's soul is in pain in the neighborhood, the pastor will tend to them and teach others how to do so. The pastor will teach people in the dotted circle how to visit the hurting ones in the local hospital. The fivefold gifting (and all the other gifts) will flow into the world. The only difference will be that in our pastoring, teaching, and evangelizing in the half circles, we can't assume beforehand the authority of Jesus will be received.

Lindsey, a woman in one of our churches, was present in the half circles of her neighborhood. She volunteered a couple nights a week at a domestic abuse shelter. Being present there, she observed great things happening. Women at the shelter asked for a Bible study. There was a great need for counselors and families to take in women. Lindsey's house group, a table fellowship of Christians in her neighborhood, recognized her gift and what was happening. They appealed for resources and help from the wider church community. From Lindsey's dotted circle fellowship, gifted people then flowed into the half circle of her life.

If Lindsey's church had been hierarchically organized, and this ministry had not fit the vision of the senior pastor, the request most likely would have been rejected, or perhaps Lindsey would have been urged to bring the ministry into the church building. But her church community was not structured like that. Instead, she was blessed by the church, and her ministry flourished with the help and coordination of others in her church. Three other people who had a passion for women in domestic abuse came alongside her. One of the women, an apostle, helped galvanize a vision for the church to get behind this work. One of the women, a pastor, came alongside Lindsey to minister healing. Some much-needed funds helped the organization take on more victims. The ministry flourished, and the church saw people added to the kingdom. The gifted structure of the church therefore is meant for all three circles. The fivefold ministry empowers people on the streets to do the ministry of the kingdom. Thus Christ's authority and reign flourishes in all the circles of our lives.

RECOVERING FAITHFUL PRESENCE AMONG OUR LEADERS

It is evident through history the church gradually removed leadership from the neighborhoods and house churches and moved it into a clerical hierarchy once it became dominant in Rome. One could argue this move was necessary for sustaining the church in the midst of huge growth. Nonetheless, I would argue, an intensification of hierarchy in the church is a symptom of the maintenance mode. Hierarchy almost always works to take leadership out of neighborhoods and center the church in a building. It organizes the church for efficiency, not for mission.

In most evangelical Protestant churches, we function as hierarchies. And no matter how servant-driven the leadership might be, there's an assumed distance between the leader and those being led. For most evangelical Protestants this understanding of leadership drives how we organize and lead churches. It is leadership that runs on efficiency—the maintenance mode—as opposed to the presence, power, and authority of Jesus Christ in our midst.

When we forfeit mutuality and tending to the presence of Christ among leadership, we forfeit the practice of the fivefold ministry as well. We forfeit dependence on the Spirit and God filling and using our gifts. We in effect lose the authority and power of Christ to reign among us. We lose the centrifugal force pushing the authority and power of ministry into the neighborhoods. When we reach this point, the church defaults into either maintenance mode or exhaustion.

Throughout the history of the church in the West, attempts have been made to recover the fivefold ministry and the multitude of the gifts. For instance, in the Middle Ages monastic orders arose to fulfill one or more of the giftings of the Holy Spirit in the world as the church lumbered on in maintenance mode. During the Radical Reformation, many Anabaptist and Brethren groups sought to return to the priesthood of all believers. And John Wesley organized society meetings of laypeople in the Second Great Awakening. True renewal, it seems, always starts with local communities of pluralized leadership fostering grassroots movements. This points to the urgency of recovering the practice of the fivefold ministry throughout all the circles of life, which will shape the church's faithful presence in the world.

SEVEN

KINGDOM PRAYER

The drive for control is at the core of the human condition. We live daily with overwhelming uncertainties. Anxiety is the air we breathe in the Western economies. Most people live isolated, vulnerable lives, and so we strive as individuals to secure our existence in every way. We live under the delusion that we are in control of our lives. As a result, endless striving characterizes our existence. Most of us are not aware of how much it's affecting us physically and emotionally.

God can't work amid our striving. Certainly he works around us and despite us. He is still ultimately sovereign and in control of the world. But as for actually using us in his power and authority, he will not oppose our grabbing and pushing for control. He refuses to steamroll our wills in order to dictate his will in our lives and in the world. God is love. God is patient. God's power can only work through us as we submit to him, let him work, open up space for him. As we gather in his presence, submit to him, and tend to his presence, he then works in all his power.

The apostle Paul challenges the Philippians, "Do not be anxious about anything, but in every situation, by prayer and petition, with thanksgiving, present your requests to God" (Phil 4:6 NIV). Prayer is the opposite of striving and anxiousness. Therefore, in everything we are to resist striving and instead present ourselves before God in prayer. Paul actually separates prayer from petition, putting it first. Prayer, as we will discover, is the profound act of giving up control of a situation, turning it over to the reign of God. Only after we have entered this space can we ask for things. Prayer opens space for his kingdom and for us to participate in his kingdom. I call this practice kingdom prayer.

THE NEED FOR KINGDOM PRAYER

Kingdom prayer is the foundation for all the other practices. It initiates all the other practices. Through prayer we approach the Lord's Table, begin reconciliation, proclaim the gospel, be with the least of these, and do all of the other practices. It is ubiquitous. And so some might wonder, *Should it be treated as a separate practice that shapes us into his faithful presence? Shouldn't it be integrated into all of the other practices?* I suggest otherwise. It is so important that we must separate it from the other practices and treat it all on its own.

Kingdom prayer gathers us into Christ's presence. It creates this local space for God's kingdom to come "on earth as it is in heaven." Historically, it has initiated (in some way) all the sacraments. It sets the stage for Christ's presence to become visible. In this way it's a social sacrament.

THE PRACTICE OF KINGDOM PRAYER

The practice of kingdom prayer is given to us by Christ most directly and obviously in the Lord's Prayer (Mt 6:9-13). Here Jesus teaches us how to pray by starting with the address, "Our Father." It is not an individualist "*My* Father." It joins people into a social group in submission to God together with "*Our* Father." It gathers a circle of subjects in submission to God's reign. Right up front we learn that kingdom prayer is a social practice. "Our Father" alerts us that to pray the kingdom prayer is a profoundly political act, joining us together as a group ready to disrupt the forces of evil in the world.

"Our Father" therefore resists the propensity in the modern West to reduce prayer to something intensely personal only. In praying this prayer, we are diverted away from focusing on the things *I* long for and desire. We must cease this striving first before we petition God.

We address God as our Father who is "in heaven." We bow before him as the one sitting at the seat of all authority in heaven and on earth. This prayer gathers *us* to be with him in submission to his authority, not only over our lives but the entire world.

Jesus then instructs us to say, "Let your name be holy." By praying this we not only acknowledge that God is sovereign, working over the whole earth, but that he can be trusted to be perfect in every way. By praying "let your name be holy," we are submitting to him so space can be opened for his perfect ways to be made manifest in our midst.

The next words, "Your kingdom come, your will be done, on earth as it is in heaven," guide our hearts, minds, and souls into a joining together in order to submit to the King. We are in essence pledging to cooperate with God. Our hearts are purified before God. Our attention is guided by this prayer to his power, majesty, grace, and authority. And a space is opened up for him to work. This kind of kingdom prayer is the most foundational of all practices for our faithful presence to God in the world.

All our other concerns for provisions and safety and forgiveness flow from here. As we are formed by his will over our lives, all of our desires become shaped by him. We are able to see the needs before us with trust in him. We see ourselves as part of God's mission. We then are able to pray for needs, including our own, like we never have before.

This is what kingdom prayer does. Together we bow before the King. We submit our lives, resources, and situations to his reign. His reign becomes a social reality. It creates the social space for his presence. It opens the way for his kingdom to break in. It enables us to participate in his work. It shapes us together for mission. It is the founding practice that constitutes his people into his faithful presence.

CHRIST'S PRESENCE

Romans 8:15-17 also teaches us to pray, "Father." Here, however, in the most intimate of ways, the apostle uses the word for "Daddy" as our address to the Father. Paul, most likely using Jesus' very own word for *father* in the original Aramaic, says we cry "*Abba*, Father." In so doing, Paul says the Spirit himself bears witness with our spirit that we indeed are children of the Father, "heirs of God and joint heirs with Christ" (v. 17). In prayer, we are joined with the Spirit. It is the entry way into his presence. But in this text prayer is more than an individual ecstatic experience.

Theologian Sarah Coakley uses Romans 8 to describe prayer as drawing us into the center of the triune God (vv. 26-27). She discusses the posture of vulnerability that enables us to submit entirely into the workings of God. Prayer is not just a contemplative experience that extracts us out of the world.[1] Rather, in prayer, we are joined with the whole work of God as all of creation is being taken up into this flow of his presence (vv. 21-22). For Coakley, submission to God through prayer incorporates us into the presence of God at the center of the triune fellowship, but it does not stop there. The triune God is at work in the world. Being shaped into his presence therefore shapes us to be immersed in his work in and for the world. This is why I call it kingdom prayer.

We practice it in all situations of life. When we encounter a domestic violence issue in the neighborhood, race and hatred at the town hall, or a sick family struggling with multiple ailments, we gather around this space, join hands, and pray, and we in essence submit this social space to Christ's presence. The kingdom is not only subjects, it's space and time, systems and realities that shape how we live. By joining together in these spaces and praying "Your kingdom come," we are opening space for his presence to become visible. Where his presence becomes manifest, violence is resisted and sickness is covered by his lordship. We now become free and present to join in God's work to reconcile this situation to himself. The Spirit is invoked. People are healed. The dying are emboldened. Violence is dissipated. Evil is defeated. Far from only personal and contemplative, praying "your kingdom come, your will be done" opens up social space to participate in what God is doing.

In 2010 a group of eight people from two Sacramento churches felt called to the Detroit Boulevard neighborhood of Sacramento. It was known as one of the most notorious crime-ridden neighborhoods in all of Sacramento. Each house in that neighborhood was a place of danger. Nonetheless, this group of eight decided to walk through the neighborhood praying over each home and praying for the presence of Christ to reign over violence, addiction, and satanic oppression. One of the eight, Sacramento street detective Michael Xiong reported that "each time we prayed over the houses, we felt the weight of oppression becoming lighter." A woman from one of the houses confronted them. When she discovered they were praying for the community, she asked for healing, and God healed her.

The group soon physically moved into the neighborhood and started what they called Detroit Life Church. A couple years later the *Sacramento Bee* reported that there were no homicides, robberies, or sex crimes and only one assault in Detroit Boulevard between 2013 and 2014. Detroit Boulevard had been transformed by a small group of people who began their ministry in the neighborhood by praying around houses, streets, and parks for the power of Satan to be vanquished.[2] Kingdom prayer embodies what it means to be faithfully present to his presence in the world.

THE ORDERING OF THE KINGDOM IN PRAYER

Order always comes with the kingdom. In this space of kingdom prayer, God reorders lives and the world by his lordship. As in Detroit Boulevard, this ordering begins when, in prayer, we have given up control and submitted ourselves to his lordship, and prepared ourselves to participate in his work, not ours. Kingdom prayer disciplines us into giving up control and cooperating with what God is doing.

Nowhere is this better illustrated than in a text from the Gospel of Mark. In Mark 9:14-29 Jesus is descending the Mount of Transfiguration with three of his disciples. When they arrive at the bottom, they discover a commotion. A man in the crowd tells Jesus that he brought his son, who was robbed of his speech by a spirit, to the disciples. He reports that the disciples failed to heal the boy. Jesus sighs, calls the disciples "faithless," and then heals the boy. Later, after all the commotion is over, the frustrated disciples ask him, "Why couldn't we drive it out?" to which Jesus replies, "This kind can come out only by prayer" (vv. 28-29 NIV).

Here we see that the disciples were still under the spell that the kingdom is something humans can bring in. They asked, in essence, how come *we* couldn't cast out this spirit? They believed it was within their power and authority to do so. After calling them faithless, Jesus refers them to the posture of prayer in which they submit this situation to God's reign. Jesus is challenging them to submit all things to God's work, trust him, and walk in that. In so doing, God will not only accomplish the kingdom but enable us to participate with him in bringing in his kingdom. This is the foundation of faithful presence.

As we walk through our neighborhoods, as we see the struggles and strife in the hallways of our schools, as we engage the hurting people around tables in McDonald's and other restaurants, as we face racial conflict on our city blocks, as we feel the resistance to God's ways and his kingdom in all these things, we should first gather with someone and pray. Submit these places and situations to the kingdom for God's work and then participate faithfully as the Spirit manifests Christ's presence. We should discern how to respond, realizing that we have been invited into the presence of Christ's work in reordering the world. And even though suffering and pain might ensue, we know that as God has used the cross to rearrange the world, so too will he use us (and our walking through the suffering) to rearrange people's lives—and whole towns and villages—as visible realities of his kingdom.

I once heard Charles Galbreath, a pastor of Clarendon Road Church in Brooklyn, tell the story of a black man gunned down by police in his neighborhood. Anger seethed in the neighborhood. Frustration from years of racial oppression was about to erupt in violence. Many people lined up to march down the main street while police gathered, expecting violence. Charles and a group of pastors rushed to the gathering place and found themselves caught in the middle between the police and the people. Tensions were rising. Insults were being hurled across the divide. One side picked up rocks, the other side clutched their guns.

The pastors feared for their lives; bullets could fly at any moment. He says that some of the pastors bowed in the middle of the street and began to pray. They implored God to visit this place. As Charles tells it, slowly the tension died down, the people put down the rocks, and the police took their hands off their holsters. Those who cared stayed. And without a shot fired or rock thrown, conversations began and God's presence appeared that night in that community. It was the beginning of something new God was doing to bring justice and reconciliation to a street corner.[3]

Kingdom prayer does not remove us from the world but places us firmly in the middle of it. Even in the most violent, awkward, and hopeless circumstances, kingdom prayer opens space for God's presence and strengthens those praying to walk faithfully in that presence. His presence calms human striving, anger, violence, and the urge to control. And then, with the way made clear, we can cooperate with God's work to realign human realities. We can participate in bringing the kingdom, whether through reconciliation, the gospel, reorienting economic realities, or any of the other seven practices of faithful presence.

After praying "Your kingdom come," we can begin the work of responding to and joining in with what God is doing. Just as the petitions of the Lord's Prayer ask for horizontal needs like forgiveness, daily bread, and shelter from the evil one, so too we can pray for these things as we stand in the middle of life's circumstances with others. Kingdom prayer prepares space for this work. It disrupts evil and makes space for reordering life.

IN ALL THE CIRCLES OF OUR LIVES

We most easily learn how to pray kingdom prayer together with Christians. In the close circle we gather together intently as one people submitted to one Lord and one table. We are already committed to discern the kingdom. But of course kingdom prayer must not be sequestered among Christians in our church meetings. We must continually practice kingdom prayer as groups in our neighborhoods and as individuals representing our communities wherever we inhabit the half circles of our lives. Prayer is a natural response to the struggles and pains we engage together as a people in everyday life.

Following Scot McKnight, I suggest we should allow the exact words of the Lord's Prayer to shape our prayer together in the world.[4] The first two petitions, which I have focused on in this chapter, set the stage for the rest of the petitions regarding daily life. In teaching the Lord's Prayer this way, Jesus is urging us to start off every prayer with the submission of our life and desires to the kingdom, from which our prayer life and petitions flow. The vertical sets the stage for the horizontal.[5]

As McKnight and others note, it was common for Jews to pray at regular intervals throughout the day.[6] Prayer was to be part of everyday life, not just early mornings or on the sabbath. In the modern world we may no longer pray at set hours. Yet what drives the practice of the hours applies to today. Kingdom prayer penetrates all the situations and encounters of our daily lives. We need to practice it in all the circles of our lives. We need to live within the frame of kingdom prayer. We should continually gather and submit all these into the space of God's inbreaking kingdom.

Every Friday night in my home, our gathering in the neighborhood would end with us joining in the living room with our children to submit all the things we had shared to Christ's reign. Even with strangers in our midst, we would pray, though we would sometimes ask their permission. As on-lookers, they saw the kingdom breaking in. This was kingdom prayer in the dotted circle.

Likewise kingdom prayer shapes our presence in the half circles of our lives. I once listened to a group of pastors speaking on the topic of evan-gelism at a small conference. One pastor told us how the simplest and easiest thing to do when he meets someone in the midst of struggle, pain, un-certainty, or need is to offer to pray. Even if this person is a stranger, this pastor said the invitation to pray was rarely turned down. For him, prayer was the door that opens space for a conversation, an encounter with God, and opportunities to pro-claim the gospel to those who are hurting and in pain.

In the case of being with a stranger, however, we must always offer kingdom prayer as a guest in that person's life. In the half circles of our lives we must always be ready to offer kingdom prayer, but never coerce it on someone. We must not be too quick to offer kingdom prayer. To simply spring prayer on someone as a tool to get them to an evangelistic moment is a mistake. There must be a connection. We must be present to the other person and to Christ's presence at work. Prayer is not contextless. True kingdom prayer demands we know and are involved in a situation concretely enough that an actual space is formed by our joining in prayer together. Here in this space we submit real situations to his lordship.

RECOVERING FAITHFUL PRESENCE
THROUGH KINGDOM PRAYER

Throughout its history the church has been tempted to limit corporate prayer to within the four walls of the church building. For example, in many churches the pastoral prayer is prayed *for* the congregation instead of *by* the congregation. Some may point to the weekly prayer meeting as an example of this. Although started in the nineteenth century to spur revivals, sometimes this well-meaning program took prayer out of the neighborhoods and sequestered it in the four walls of the church on a Wednesday night.

Whenever the church relinquishes prayer to the professionals, or whenever the church removes prayer from the places of tension, need, and struggle in all three circles of our lives, kingdom prayer is in danger of becoming a maintenance function of the church. We must guard against this.

Life on the Vine practiced kingdom prayer in Sunday gatherings by asking the people to audibly voice their prayers to God in two to three sentences. Everyone was asked to end their prayer with "Lord, in your mercy." When the congregation heard that, we would all join in unison with, "Amen." This was our way of submitting our needs to the Father's care and then agreeing on it together as a community. We were continually and intentionally led into the concrete submission that is kingdom prayer. And so this space became sacred space for the kingdom. It was training for kingdom prayer in our daily lives.

When there is no kingdom prayer in the half circles of our lives, this raises red flags that perhaps the church has slipped into exhaustion mode. If prayer opens us to what God is doing among us in these various places of our lives, our entrance into these places should be prepared for by kingdom prayer.

Today many churches are learning the value of prayer walks in their neighborhoods (much like the church in Detroit Boulevard). Walking our neighborhoods and going to places of strife and then joining hands in solidarity and praying "Your kingdom come" opens space for Christ to be made visible. In similar fashion, I know friends who marched arm in arm in the midst of violence in Chicago, praying "Your kingdom come." Kingdom prayer is spatial and social. It opens spaces and extends Christ's presence into our neighborhoods. In these spaces, when people submit to Christ's presence, Christ's power is unleashed. Healings, reconciliation, and peace break out in Jesus' name. And the world looks on in wonder, asking what has made such happenings possible. These things are not possible by human effort.

Too often we come to prayer believing the more we pray the more results we will see. This too is a sign the church has slipped into exhaustion mode. Even with the best of intentions, we can gather merely to pray for the implementation of our own quick solutions to a situation of social injustice, for instance. Prayer has become in effect a quick-fix means to exhaustion. Jesus counters this propensity before he introduces the Lord's Prayer by instructing, "When you are praying, do not heap up empty phrases as the Gentiles do; for they think that they will be heard because of their many words" (Mt 6:7). Our God is sovereign, holy, and firmly in charge of the world. He is waiting to invite us to participate in his work. So prayer's primary task is to align us with God and his purposes. It brings us into a relationship in which we become participants in his work to change the world.

From this space we offer our needs, desires, and prayers for protection, just as children do to their parents. Then we add our deepest desires to our prayer. Likewise, we respond to the injustices that so anger our souls. We plead for God to make things right, and space is opened up for Christ's kingdom to break in with power and authority.

It's just as true with kingdom prayer as it is with all the other practices, both maintenance and exhaustion are a denial of Christ's presence. They fail to open space for God to work. The practice of kingdom prayer undercuts both modes. Kingdom prayer is the ground of all the practices. Recovering it is the foundation of the church's faithful presence in the world.

And so it is fitting we end this outline of the seven practices with kingdom prayer. It is not only the foundation of all the other practices, it is the foundation for living the entire Christian life. It guides us into submitting ourselves to Christ and opening up space for his presence among us. It embodies the posture by which we gather at every meal, in every conflict, while proclaiming the gospel, while sitting with the marginalized, being with children, and exercising his gifts. It shapes us to live as his faithful presence in the world. Only as we pray "Thy kingdom come" can we truly participate in his work in all these ways. For this is the way God has chosen to change the world.

NOTES

1 THE LORD'S TABLE

[1]Although I developed the three circles concept out of my own church leadership, the idea of three circles or three different spaces for the meal is not without precedent. See Andrew B. McGowan, *Ancient Christian Worship* (Grand Rapids: Baker Academic, 2014), 50-51; and Russell E. Riche, "Family Meal, Holy Communion, and Love Feats: Three Ecumenical Metaphors," in *Ecumenical and Interreligious Perspectives* (Nashville: Quarterly Review of Books, 1992), 17-29.

[2]Henri de Lubac, *Corpus Mysticum: The Eucharist and the Church in the Middle Ages* (Notre Dame, IN: University of Notre Dame Press, 2006).

2 RECONCILIATION

[1]Martin Luther King Jr., "Letter from Birmingham Jail," published as "The Negro Is Your Brother," *Atlantic Monthly* 212, no. 2 (1963): 78-88.

3 PROCLAIMING THE GOSPEL

[1]I follow here Scot McKnight, *King Jesus Gospel* (Grand Rapids: Zondervan, 2012), among others, including N. T. Wright.

[2]Even though the proclaimer always maintains a posture as one among, they preach the gospel *over* the church as an all-engrossing reality to be accepted or rejected.

4 BEING WITH
THE "LEAST OF THESE"

[1]I heard this story firsthand from the pastor at a "Cultivate Learning Party" put on by Pernell Goodyear in London, Ontario.

[2]Samuel Wells, *God's Companions: Reimagining Christian Ethics* (Oxford: Blackwell, 2006), 7.

[3]A. M. Henry, *Christ in His Sacraments* (Chicago: Fides, 1958), 279.

5 BEING WITH CHILDREN

[1]This storytelling method first developed by Anglicans in London has spread around the world. See the Godly Play website at www.godlyplay.org.

6 THE FIVEFOLD GIFTING

[1]Many of these tests are available. The one I have found most helpful is in an appendix of Mike Breen's *Building a Discipleship Culture*, 2nd ed. (Pawleys Island, SC: 3DM Publishing, 2014).

7 KINGDOM PRAYER

[1]Sarah Coakley, "Why Three? Some Further Reflections on the Origins of the Doctrine of the Trinity," in *The Making and Remaking of Christian Doctrine*, ed. Sarah

Coakley and David A. Pailin (Oxford: Clarendon Press, 1993).

[2]Michael C. Xiong, "The Presence of God," *Alliance Life*, July-August 2015, www.cmalliance.org/alife/the-presence-of-god.

[3]I heard Charles tell this story at the Global Impact conference of the Metro District, Christian and Missionary Alliance, New Jersey, February 20–21, 2015, where he spoke. I tell this story as best I can recall it and do not hold Charles responsible for the accuracy of all the details.

[4]Scot McKnight, *Sermon on the Mount*, Story of God Bible Commentary (Grand Rapids: Zondervan, 2013), 174.

[5]McKnight uses these words to describe the two parts of Lord's Prayer (ibid., 173).

[6]Ibid., 188-90.

 **Missio Alliance**

and

≋ INTERVARSITY PRESS

Missio Alliance has arisen in response to the shared voice of pastors and ministry leaders from across the landscape of North American Christianity for a new "space" of togetherness and reflection amid the issues and challenges facing the church in our day. We are united by a desire for a fresh expression of evangelical faith, one significantly informed by the global evangelical family. Lausanne's Cape Town Commitment, "A Confession of Faith and a Call to Action," provides an excellent guidepost for our ethos and aims.

In partnership with InterVarsity Press, we are pleased to offer a line of resources authored by a diverse range of theological practitioners. The resources in this series are selected based on the important way in which they address and embody these values, and thus, the unique contribution they offer in equipping Christian leaders for fuller and more faithful participation in God's mission.

Available Titles

The Church as Movement by JR Woodward and Dan White Jr., 978-0-8308-4133-2

Emboldened by Tara Beth Leach, 978-0-8308-4524-8

Embrace by Leroy Barber, 978-0-8308-4471-5

Faithful Presence by David E. Fitch, 978-0-8308-4127-1

God Is Stranger by Krish Kandiah, 978-0-8308-4532-3

Paradoxology by Krish Kandiah, 978-0-8308-4504-0

Redeeming Sex by Debra Hirsch, 978-0-8308-3639-0

Seven Practices for the Church on Mission by David E. Fitch, 978-0-8308-4142-4

White Awake by Daniel Hill, 978-0-8308-4393-0

missioalliance.org | twitter.com/missioalliance | facebook.com/missioalliance